*A Pictorial History of the Confederacy*

# A Pictorial History of the Confederacy

John Chandler Griffin

McFarland & Company, Inc., Publishers
*Jefferson, North Carolina, and London*

LIBRARY OF CONGRESS CATALOGUING-IN-PUBLICATION DATA

Griffin, John Chandler, 1936–
A pictorial history of the Confederacy / John Chandler Griffin.
p.    cm.
Includes index.

ISBN 0-7864-1744-7 (illustrated case binding : 50# alkaline paper)

1.  United States — History — Civil War, 1861–1865 — Campaigns.
2. Confederate States of America — History.    3.  Confederate States of
America — Biography.    4.  United States — History — Civil War, 1861–
1865 — Biography.    5.  United States — History — Civil War, 1861–
1865 — Campaigns — Pictorial works.    6.  Confederate States of
America — History — Pictorial works.   I.  Title.
E470.G815   2004          973.7'3 — dc22          2004003506

British Library cataloguing data are available

*Cover art:* General Thomas J. "Stonewall" Jackson *(National Archives)*

Manufactured in the United States of America

*McFarland & Company, Inc., Publishers
Box 611, Jefferson, North Carolina 28640
www.mcfarlandpub.com*

To my great-grandfather,
Pvt. John Thomas Stone,
Company H, Fifth South Carolina Cavalry Regiment,

and to the tens of thousands of other young men just like
him who left the warmth and comfort of their homes to
journey to far-off battlefields— to suffer the pangs of loneliness,
hunger, cold, terrible wounds and even death.
It was inevitable that they
would lose in the end,
but they fought all the way.

# Acknowledgments

First, my deepest appreciation goes to Dr. John Catalano, an old friend and the dean of the College at University of South Carolina–Lancaster, for putting the facilities of the university at my disposal while I worked on this volume. Over the past thirty years I've worked for numerous deans, some good, some bad, and some in-between. But John Catalano is by large measure the best, a man who is far more concerned with what he can bring to his position than what his position can bring to him.

As for our academic dean, Ron Cox, he sort of burst on the scene in the fall of 2002 and immediately established himself as an ace administrator and an all-around nice guy. His roots run deep in this Southland of ours, and his interest and assistance in the completion of this book will long be remembered.

And many thanks to Linda Guess of our Medford Library for her tireless assistance in keeping my research on the right track.

And what would I have done without the help of Blake Faulkenberry, our super computer wizard, and Shana Funderburk, our lovely PR person, who guided me through some truly puzzling spots on my computer. I am definitely not a technology person, and Blake and Shana demonstrated remarkable patience in showing me how to make the computer do what I wanted it to.

But most of all, thanks to my wife, Betty Griffin, for her understanding while my concern for this work, on far too many occasions, totally occupied my mind — often when it shouldn't have. And the same is true for my daughter, Alexis Griffin Ballard, and my two granddaughters, Emmalee Grace and Serrah Roxanne. I love them dearly, and now I can devote more attention to them and *Sesame Street* and less to the wild antics of Nathan Bedford Forrest.

Also, I wish to thank the following individuals and institutions for their assistance with securing the images in this work: Joseph H. Crute, author of *Emblems of Valor*; Devereaux Cannon, author of *Flags of the Confederacy*; the good folks at the *Civil War Times Illustrated*; David Reel of the West Point Museum; James Taylor of the Cherokee Museum; Joe Williams of the Appomattox Court House Historical Park; Nancy Sherbert of the Kansas State Historical Society; Eric Blevins of the North Carolina Division of Archives and History; Susan Dick of the Georgia Historical Society (Savannah); Vaughan Stanley of Washington & Lee University; Allen Stokes of the South Caroliniana Library of the University of South Carolina; Dale Powers of the St. Albans Historical Society; Dr. Nola Knouse of the Moravian Music Foundation; Peter Herrington of the Anne Brown Military Collection, Brown University;

Jane Yates of The Citadel Archives; Col. Diane Jacob of the Virginia Military Institute Archives; Ed Finney of the the Naval Historical Center; Megin Newman of the Lexington Foundation's Stonewall Jackson House; the Old Court House Museum, Vicksburg; David Jackson of the Jackson County Historical Society; Ginger Peterman of the Virginia State Library; the Oklahoma Historical Society; Clinton Welch of the Missouri State Historical Society; Tracie Evans of the Texas Ranger Hall of Fame and Museum, Waco; Teresa Roane of the Valentine Museum; Jeff Ruggles of the Virginia Historical Society; Heather Milne of the Confederate Museum, Richmond; Carol Potts and Melissa Faulkner of the Birmingham Museum of Art; Scott Harris of the New Market Battlefield Historical Park; Ruth Mitchell of the Maryland Historical Society; John Bigham of the South Carolina Confederate Relic Room; Pat Ricci of the Confederate Museum, New Orleans; and the good folks at both the Library of Congress and the National Archives.

# Contents

# Introduction

Even today, after the passage of some 140 years, it would be difficult to find a southerner so faint of heart that he still does not thrill at the mere mention of such august names as Robert E. Lee, Stonewall Jackson, Jubal Early, Nathan Bedford Forest, A. P. Hill or Jeb Stuart, gallant names that continue to echo down the dimly lit corridors of time. Indeed, our fascination with the Confederacy and its heroes, rather than diminishing with time, seems to have grown increasingly strong. Such being the case, for this volume I have featured a wide selection of rarely seen photos of those immortal heroes, along with details of their military careers and personal lives that are but little known to the average reader.

This book also features descriptions of more than 40 major battles of the War Between the States, along with battle maps which illustrate where the Confederates and their Union opponents were located during these various fights. Certainly it is revealing to note that in the early days of the war the Confederates were outnumbered two to one. As the months and years went by, the odds against them became even greater. Soldiers from both the North and South were dying by the thousands, but the North had a ready supply of replacements (many of them immigrants from Germany and Ireland) and the ranks of their fallen were quickly filled. Not so in the South. After 1863 when a Confederate soldier fell it was unlikely that another lad would soon take his place, for there were no lads left. Indeed, by 1864 the Confederacy was drafting boys of 17 and men of 55. These soldiers were rarely given uniforms but wore whatever civilian clothing they could bring from home. They were also urged to bring their own horses and firearms, for the Confederacy, with its ports now blockaded, had none left to issue them. As for footwear, it is interesting to observe in these old photographs of soldiers recently killed in battle that often the dead are not wearing shoes. The explanation for that is both simple and grim: the shoeless southern soldiers would generally go out after a fight and search among the dead for shoes that might fit them. As for food, by 1864 even hardtack was considered a rare delicacy.

Still, somehow, despite the military experts' opinions that the South could not last another day, the Confederate soldiers continued to fight on and on and to give good accounts of themselves, although they were by 1864 generally outnumbered three or four to one.

This book is also the story of Confederate flags. For nowhere can one find better symbols of the dogged courage displayed by these young gallants through four long years of hardship and sacrifice than in these battered, blood stained banners.

1

The poorly fed and ill-equipped Confederate army, still reputed to be one of the greatest infantries the world has ever known, defended their families and homes to the bitter end against a very large and well-equipped army. Why were they so determined? What were they fighting for? Why were they so eager to suffer and die for the South? In reality, it had nothing to do with such issues as states' rights or the institution of slavery (according to the census of 1860, 90 percent of southerners did not own slaves and had never owned slaves). Perhaps these issues motivated Jefferson Davis and the South's wealthy plantation owners, but what motivated the soldiers who actually went out and did the fighting was very simple: they were desperate to protect their homes and families from an invading federal army, an army that showed little mercy to the civilian populations.

# 1

# 1860–1861
## Secession to Fort Sumter

*Any people anywhere, being inclined and having the power, have the right to rise up and shake off the existing government, and form a new one that suits them better. This is a most valuable, a most sacred right — a right which we hope and believe is to liberate the world. Nor is this right confined to cases in which the whole people of an existing government may choose to exercise it. Any portion of such people, that can, may revolutionize, and make their own of so much of the territory as they inhabit.*

— Abraham Lincoln, January 12, 1848

On October 1, 1860, some two months prior to the national election, Governor William Henry Gist of South Carolina could already see the grim writing on the wall. The national Democratic party had been split; the northern faction was in favor of Stephen A. Douglas, while the southerners were in favor of John C. Breckinridge, thereby ensuring the election of Abraham Lincoln, the candidate of the Black Republicans, to the office of president of the United States. Gist remembered only too well Lincoln's campaign speech of 1858 ("A House Divided"), back when he was running for the senate from Illinois, when he warned that the spread of slavery must be immediately checked and eventually abolished: "In my opinion, it will not cease, until a crisis shall have been reached and passed. A house divided against itself cannot stand. I believe this government cannot endure, permanently half slave and half free. I do not expect the Union to be dissolved — I do not expect the house to fall — but I do expect it will cease to be divided. It will become all one thing, or all the other. Either the opponents of slavery will arrest the further spread of it, and place it where the public mind shall rest in the belief that it is in course of ultimate extinction; or its advocates will push it forward, till it shall become alike lawful in all the states, old as well as new — North as well as South."

Lincoln's intentions were clear. Should he become president, he would abolish slavery throughout the nation.

Gist immediately wrote letters to the governors of twelve other southern states asking if they would join South Carolina in considering seceding from the Union should Lincoln be elected. "If you decide to call a convention," Gist wrote, "upon the election of a majority of electors favorable to Lincoln, I desire to know the day you propose for the meeting, that we may call our convention to meet the same day, if possible."

And, of course, Gist was quite correct. On November 6 Lincoln received 1,866,452 votes out of the 4,682,069 total cast. His was a minority victory, but in the Electoral College Lincoln received 180 votes against 123 for his three opponents.

By November 6 Governor Gist had already received replies to his letters urging immediate action. Typical is the response he received from Florida's Governor M. S. Perry: "I am proud to say that Florida is ready to wheel into line with the gallant Palmetto State, or any other Cotton State or States, in any course which she or they may in their judgement think proper to adopt. If there is sufficient manliness in the South to strike for our rights, honor, and safety, in God's name let it be done before the inauguration of Lincoln."

South Carolina wasted no time. On December 18 the delegates to the Secession Convention met in Charleston and passed by a unanimous vote an ordinance of secession, stating: "…the union subsisting between South Carolina and the other States, under the name of 'The United States of America,' is hereby dissolved."

As the new year got underway other southern states began to join South Carolina in her bid for independence: Mississippi on January 9; Florida on January 10; Alabama on January 11; Georgia on January 26; and Texas on February 1.

On February 4 delegates from these states met in Montgomery, Alabama, to form a provisional government. They adopted a constitution modeled after that of the United States, and provided for raising 100,000 volunteers to serve for a period of twelve months. These states also gave to the Confederacy property of the national government (such as arsenals and forts) which they had already seized.

On February 9 the Confederate Congress chose Jefferson Davis president and Alexander Stephens vice president. They would be sworn in on March 4.

That same day, some eight hundred miles to the northeast, Abraham Lincoln was being inaugurated in Washington, D.C. His speech, for the most part, was conciliatory, though he sounded an ominous note at the end when he stated: "The power confided in me, will be used to hold, occupy, and possess the property, and places belonging to the government; but beyond what may be necessary for these objects, there will be no invasion — no using of force against, or among the people anywhere."

To General Winfield Scott, commander of the U.S. Army, Lincoln had days earlier sent the following message: "I shall be obliged to you to be as well prepared as you can to either *hold*, or *retake*, the forts, as the case may require, at, and after the inauguration."

This, of course, did not bode well for the South, for as each state seceded, its troops had seized nearly all the Federal forts within its boundaries or off its shores. Indeed, only four such forts remained in the hands of the Union: Fort Jefferson in the Dry Tortugas, Fort Pickens in Pensacola Bay, Fort Taylor at Key West, and Fort Sumter in Charleston Harbor. And Lincoln had just stated that he would use the power of the Federal government to hold and occupy those properties, or to *retake* them if necessary.

The southern states immediately sent commissioners to Washington to negotiate the transfer of those forts still occupied by Union forces to the Confederacy. But Lincoln refused to even meet with them. Instead, he sent a message to Governor Gist of South Carolina. It was taken by a State Department clerk, Robert S. Chew: "I am directed by the President of the United States to notify you to expect an attempt will be made to supply Fort Sumter with provisions only; and that, if such attempt be not resisted, no effort to throw in men, arms, or ammunition, will be made, without further notice, or in case of an attack upon the fort."

Francis Pickens, now governor of South Carolina, immediately relayed this message to Jefferson Davis in Montgomery. Davis and his cabinet met and agonized over just what their response should be. Finally it was decided to direct the commander of Confederate forces in Charleston, General P. G. T. Beauregard, to demand the immediate evacuation of the fort and if Major Robert Anderson refused, to take it by force.

On April 11 Beauregard met with Major Anderson and demanded the surrender of the fort. Anderson, of course, could not comply with Beauregard's order, but he did tell him that his troops had depleted their supply of food and water and thus they would be forced to evacuate the fort within forty-eight hours. In other words, Beauregard could occupy the fort

**Jefferson Davis, President of the Confederate States of America** (1807–1889). *An 1828 graduate of West Point, in 1835 Davis married Sarah Knox Taylor, the daughter of President Zachary Taylor, who died later that year. At that point Davis went into seclusion for some ten years. Then, in 1845, he married Varina Howell, an outspoken young woman who opposed both slavery and secession. He distinguished himself in the Mexican War, and was later elected to the U.S. Senate (he was a founder of the Smithsonian Institution). He preferred a military commission to political office, but he was nevertheless elected unanimously to the presidency of the Confederacy.* (National Archives)

without firing a shot if he would only wait another forty-eight hours.

But Beauregard did not wait. Indeed, some twelve hours later, at 4:30 A.M. on April 12 he ordered his howitzers to open fire.

It was this order that triggered the most tragic event in the history of this great nation, the American Civil War.

The battle lasted for thirty-three hours. Fort Sumter was badly damaged as a result of the bombardment, but not a single soldier was killed. As for Major Anderson and his force, they were allowed to evacuate the fort peacefully and to board Union ships standing at anchor in the mouth of the harbor. As a final goodwill gesture, Beauregard allowed Anderson to fire a salute to the Stars and Stripes. (Major Anderson had been Beauregard's instructor at West Point some years earlier and recalled him as probably his finest student ever.)

Still, it is interesting to speculate, to play *what if*? *What if* Jefferson Davis had agreed to wait forty-eight hours before ordering southern troops to occupy the fort?

The Union force would have departed Fort Sumter peacefully and the southerners could have occupied the fort without firing a shot. At that point, the shoe would have been on the other foot, Lincoln's foot. Then it would have been up to Abe Lincoln to decide what the Union would do about Fort Sumter. Would he have risked starting a great war just to reclaim Fort Sumter for the Union?

*Could* he have started a great war just to reclaim Fort Sumter? His top generals had already advised him that the U.S. Navy could not take Fort Sumter without the support of at least 20,000 ground troops. Unfortunately, the U.S. Army at that time had only 13,000 foot soldiers, and most of them were scattered throughout the Western territories. Certainly Lincoln could have increased the size of his army by calling for volunteers (as he did in fact do), but for what purpose? Simply to reclaim Fort Sumter?

Or, again playing *what if*, *what if* the Confederacy had allowed Federal troops to continue their occupation of Fort Sumter? After all, what real harm were they doing? It certainly posed no military threat to Charleston or the South. Jefferson Davis claimed that it posed a threat to the South's national sovereignty, an insult of sorts. But that seems a rather lame excuse for risking the entire future of the Confederacy by going to war with the United States, one of the most powerful nations on earth. It must be remembered that the Confederacy had been a reality since February of '61, and to date the Federal government had made no moves to bring the seceded states back into the Union. Certainly there had been no threats of force at that point. So why not let sleeping dogs lie? Why provoke the Federal government? Why give it an excuse to invade the newest and certainly one of the weakest nations on earth?

The author, as dedicated to the South and the Confederacy as he is, can only conclude that the South's opening fire on Fort Sumter on April 12, 1861, must go down in history as one of the most irresponsible moves ever taken by any government in the western world.

Who knows? Had the South allowed Fort Sumter to remain a Federal possession, the Confederate States of America might still be alive and well today.

**"The First Flag of Independence Raised in the South"** *(Savannah, Ga., November 8, 1860).*
*The handsome banner in this lithograph was made by one Joseph Prendergast who obviously*
*recalled an identical flag from the American Revolution, one bearing both a snake and the words*
*"Don't Tread On Me." Charles C. Jones, the mayor of Savannah and one of the orators portrayed*
*on the balcony in the upper left, in May of '61 mailed a copy of this print to his parents along*
*with the following message:*
    *"Enclosed I send a copy of a lithograph representing in a humble way the first great meet-*
*ing of the citizens of Savannah when they realized for the first time the necessities for a grand*
*revolution. The occasion has never had a parallel in the history of our city; and as an humble*
*memento of an eventful past this rude lithograph will in after years possess no ordinary interest.*
*The individual "spreading himself" with every conceivable energy and earnestness from the bal-*
*cony of the clubhouse may be Colonel Bartow or Judge Jackson; or it may be the subscriber, then*
*mayor of the city. We all spoke, using that balcony as a rostrum, on that night to the assembled*
*multitudes, who swayed to and fro on every hand like the sea lifted by the breath of the tornado.*
*We added fuel to the flame; and that meeting, it is said, contributed more to secure the secession*
*of Georgia and to confirm the revolution in adjoining Southern states than almost any other sin-*
*gle circumstance of the times. It was followed by similar demonstrations throughout the length*
*and breadth of the cotton-growing states. It evoked unmeasured surprise and condemnation from*
*the Northern press. It stayed the hands of our sister city Charleston, and gave an impulse to the*
*wave of secession which soon swept with a rapidity and a strength, indicating no returning ebb,*
*all over the land. But few copies were struck off — say a thousand — and they were widely circu-*
*lated throughout the country."* (Library of Congress)

**The South Carolina Secession Convention at work at Secession Hall in Charleston on December 18, 1860.** *Finally, they issued a resolution which stated, "We, the people of the State of South Carolina, in Convention assembled, do declare and ordain that the union now subsisting between South Carolina and other States under the name of 'The United States of America' is hereby dissolved." In quick order, then, six other states (Mississippi, Florida, Alabama, Georgia, Louisiana and Texas) followed South Carolina out of the union.* (West Point Museum, USMA)

*Sheet music published in Charleston in early 1861, featuring the Secession Convention at work.* (Library of Congress)

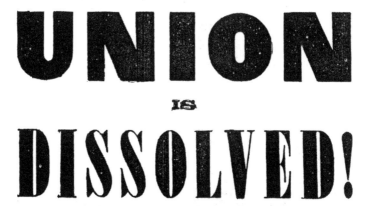

# CHARLESTON

# MERCURY

## EXTRA:

*Passed unanimously at 1.15 o'clock, P. M., December 20th, 1860.*

### AN ORDINANCE

*To dissolve the Union between the State of South Carolina and other States united with her under the compact entitled "The Constitution of the United States of America."*

We, the People of the State of South Carolina, in Convention assembled, do declare and ordain, and it is hereby declared and ordained,

That the Ordinance adopted by us in Convention, on the twenty-third day of May, in the year of our Lord one thousand seven hundred and eighty-eight, whereby the Constitution of the United States of America was ratified, and also, all Acts and parts of Acts of the General Assembly of this State, ratifying amendments of the said Constitution, are hereby repealed; and that the union now subsisting between South Carolina and other States, under the name of "The United States of America," is hereby dissolved.

## THE

# UNION

## IS

# DISSOLVED!

**Jefferson Davis and wife Varina Howell** *only days following their wedding.* (Civil War Times Illustrated Collection)

*A talented artist, Davis did this pencil drawing of the goddess Minerva while still a student at West Point. It now hangs in the West Point Museum.* (West Point Museum, USMA)

*The beautiful* **Varina Howell Davis** *as first lady of the Confederacy. Varina was an independent and highly outspoken woman who made no secret of her opposition to secession throughout the war, much to the dismay of her husband.* (National Portrait Gallery, Smithsonian Institution)

**The Davis children** *in exile in Toronto in 1866. They are (L–R): Jefferson, Jr., Margaret, Winnie and William Howell. Tragically, in 1864, the Davis' four-year-old son, Joseph, was instantly killed when he fell from a fourth-story balcony at the White House in Richmond. Of all the Davis children, only Margaret and Winnie would survive their parents.* (Library of Congress)

*Having aged terribly,* **Jefferson Davis** *was released from Fortress Monroe in 1867. He was happy to be free, but extremely disappointd that he was denied his day in court where he felt certain he could prove that the Southern states had a perfect Constitutional right to secede from the Union. He would live until 1889.*

*This photo of* **President Davis** *was taken only hours following his capture on May 10, 1865, near Irwinville, Georgia. Following two years of imprisonment, he would join his family in Toronto, Canada. They returned to America in 1868, and Davis died a peaceful death in 1889. (In 1861 the Vatican recognized the Confederacy as a free and independent nation. Following the war, with Davis now in prison, a deeply sympathetic pope, with his own hands, wove a crown of thorns which he sent to Davis. It is now on display in the Confederate Museum in Richmond.)* (Library of Congress)

JAMES A. SEDDON
Secretary of War.

CHRISTOPHER G. MEMMINGER
Secretary of the Treasury.

STEPHEN R. MALLORY
Secretary of the Navy.

JOHN H. REAGAN
Postmaster-General.

ALEXANDER H. STEPHENS
Vice-President.

JUDAH P. BENJAMIN
Secretary of State.

(Civil War Times Illustrated)

**General Samuel Cooper** *(1798–1876), the top ranking officer in the Confederate Army. A native of New Jersey, Cooper graduated from West Point in 1815. In 1841 he became adjutant general of the U.S. Army, under Secretary of War Jefferson Davis. In 1861 Davis named him adjutant general of the Confederate Army. As such, Cooper's duties were incredibly difficult, but he performed brilliantly. After the war he turned over to Union authorities the complete records of the Confederate Army, for which historians are most grateful.* (National Archives)

**Judah P. Benjamin,** *secretary of state and Davis' most trusted advisor. (He had served as a U.S. senator from Louisiana prior to the war, the first Jew elected to the U.S. Senate.) Following Lee's surrender he fled America and eventually became a highly respected London barrister.* (National Archives)

**Montgomery, Alabama,** *February 8, 1861, the day the Confederate Constitution was adopted. As can be seen from the big Capitol clock, it is now 1 p.m., just moments after Davis was sworn in as interim president of the Confederate States of America. Seen here, he is leading the spectators in prayer. This memorable photograph was made by A. C. McIntyre, a noted artist from Montgomery.* (Library of Congress)

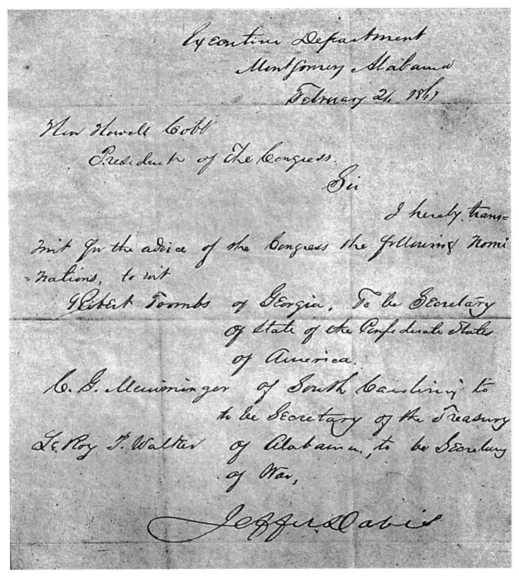

*President Jefferson Davis' first order to the Confederate Congress, submitting three names for Congress to consider as members of Davis' cabinet.* (The Confederate Museum, Richmond)

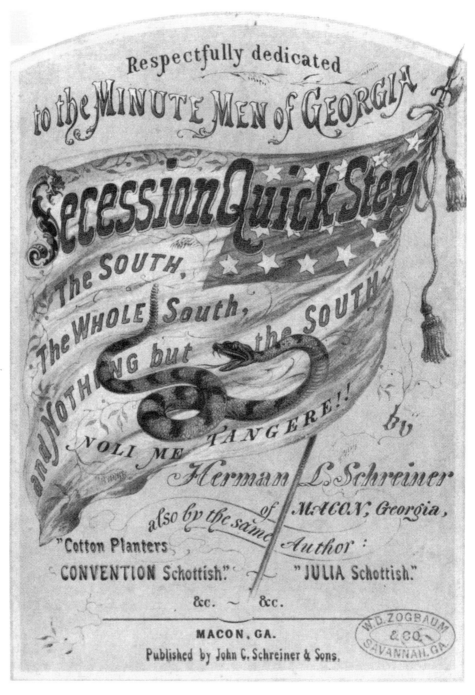

*The early months of 1861 became a time of patriotic songs, including "Secession Quick Step," written by Hermann Schreiner of Macon, Georgia, and dedicated to "the Minute Men of Georgia." It should be noted that this sheet music bears patriotic images from the American Revolution, including the Stars and Stripes. (Georgia Historical Society, Savannah)*

*Little remembered today, the Confederacy's national anthem, "God Save the South," was written by Maryland poet George H. Miles in 1862.* (Civil War Times Illustrated)

## The Bonnie Blue Flag

By the spring of 1861, as state after state followed South Carolina out of the Union, many local flags had already been unveiled across the South. Several of these, including the Palmetto Flag of South Carolina, would gain such popularity during the war that they would later be adopted as state flags.

And there was also the Bonnie Blue Flag. It featured a large white star on a blue field, and attained great popularity across the South.

Though sometimes confused with the Lone Star Flag of Texas, the Bonnie Blue Flag had been in existence since as early as 1810 when it had served as the national flag of the now-forgotten Republic of West Florida. Then in 1861 an itinerant Irish minstrel named Harry Macarthy, aware of the patriotic fervor that gripped the Con-

federacy, revived interest in this banner when he toured the southern states armed with a banjo and a rich tenor voice, thrilling audiences with his stirring rendition of *The Bonnie Blue Flag.* Not only was everyone soon humming this catchy little ditty, but militia units from Maryland to Texas were adopting the Bonnie Blue Flag as their standard. Citizens of Alabama, for example, created a Bonnie Blue Flag when they took the star that represented them in the United States flag and placed it on a plain blue field. The state flags of North Carolina, Texas and Mississippi also prominently featured a single star.

**The Bonnie Blue Flag.** (Joseph H. Crute, Jr., *Emblems of Southern Valor*)

*This sheet music featured both the Bonnie Blue Flag and the Stars and Bars.* (Music Division, New York Public Library)

### *The Bonnie Blue Flag*
By Harry Macarthy

We are a band of brothers and native to the soil,
Fighting for the property we gained by honest toil;
And when our rights were threatened, the cry rose near and far,
Hurrah for the Bonnie Blue Flag that bears a single star!

Chorus—

Hurrah! Hurrah! for Southern Rights, hurrah!
Hurrah! for the Bonnie Blue Flag that bears a Single star!

As long as the Union was faithful to her trust,
Like friends and like brothers we were kind, we Were just;
But now when Northern treachery attempts our right to mar,
We hoist on high the Bonnie Blue Flag that bears a single star.

*The members of the 26th North Carolina Regimental Band, called one of the best in the Confederacy, were all volunteers from the Moravian community in Salem, N.C. In addition to playing in the band, musicians also served as medics. During the first day's fighting at Gettysburg the 26th North Carolina suffered heavy casualties, and thus these bandsmen were up all night caring for their wounded comrades. Yet the next day they turned out to play for their fellow troops and were lustily cheered.* (The Moravian Music Foundation)

**Southern State Flags, 1860–65** (courtesy of Devereaux Cannon, *Flags of the Confederacy*).

Alabama, 1861

Louisiana, 1861

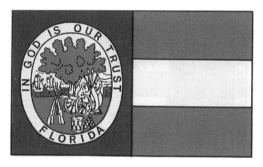

Florida, 1861

Mississippi, 1861

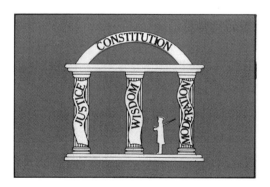

Georgia, 1861

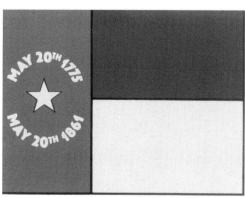

North Carolina, 1861

**Southern State Flags, 1860–65** (courtesy of Devereaux Cannon, *Flags of the Confederacy*).

*South Carolina, adopted January 26, 1861*

*Texas, January 25, 1839, to the present*

*South Carolina, January 28, 1861,*
*to the present*

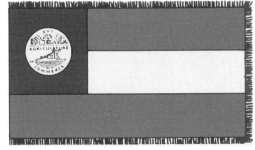

*Tennessee, 1861*

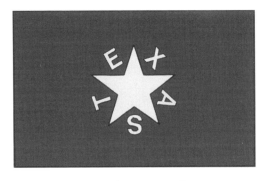

*Texas, March 11 to December 10, 1836*

*Virginia, 1861*

## The Birth of the Stars and Bars

On February 8, 1861, some two weeks prior to Jefferson Davis' swearing in ceremony, forty-three delegates from the seven seceding southern states (South Carolina, Georgia, Florida, Alabama, Mississippi, Louisiana, and Texas) met in Montgomery, in the Alabama State Senate chambers, to put the finishing touches on their plan to form a new nation, the Confederate States of America. This they did and the Confederacy suddenly became a fact of life. And Jefferson Davis, a West Point graduate and former cabinet member under President Pierce, was elected interim president.

Davis and the assembled delegates were overwhelmed with all the details involved in getting the Confederacy off the ground. First, they formulated a constitution. It was modeled after the United States Constitution, but this one spelled out very clearly the supreme rights of the individual states that comprised the Confederacy, and the right of any individual state to secede from the Confederacy should it be in that state's best interests to do so.

Davis and the delegates also appointed a committee, chaired by Colonel William Porcher Miles, to select a design for a national flag. Almost immediately citizens began to inundate the committee with suggestions and designs for the new Confederate flag. From the beginning it became obvious that the old Stars and Stripes still held tremendous appeal for most southerners, for nearly all the suggested designs were simply variations of the United States flag.

Finally, on March 4, the very day that Jefferson Davis was to take the oath of office, the committee announced that after much deliberation it had chosen a design submitted by Orren Randolph Smith of Louisburg, N.C. Predictably enough, Smith's flag retained the colors of the Stars and Stripes and used them in essentially the same manner. The new flag was to have a canton of blue containing seven white stars, one for each state of the new Confederacy. The field was composed of three broad stripes, or bars, of equal width, with the top and bottom bars being red, the middle bar white. The committee then met with the various delegates to unveil their selection, and the delegates, distracted with more serious matters, quickly approved the selection.

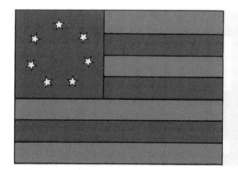 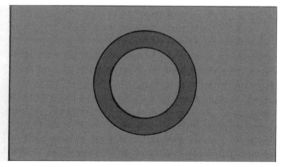

*Just two of the many handsome banners rejected by the Confederate Congress on March 4, 1861, in favor of those designs submitted by Orren Smith. (Both flags courtesy of Cannon, Flags of the Confederacy)*

This new flag was immediately dubbed the Stars and Bars.

Interestingly enough, the delegates had hoped to hoist the Stars and Bars to the top of the Capitol dome at the very moment Lincoln was delivering his inaugural address in Washington. But such an irony was not to be, unfortunately, for it was 3:30 P.M. before the seamstresses could finish sewing the new flag, hours after Lincoln had completed his speech.

But once the Stars and Bars did begin its slow ascent to the top of the State House, bedlam erupted on the grounds. Mixed in with the hurrahs of hundreds of citizens gathered for the occasion was the martial music of a dozen militia bands, and the various artillery units assembled for that momentous occasion fired off their cannons as the Stars and Bars reached its zenith.

This is how the *Mobile Daily Advertiser* described the occasion:

"At 3:30 P.M. on yesterday the flag of the Confederate States of America was flung out to the breeze from the staff on the Capital. Miss L. T. Tyler, one of the fair descendants of the Old Dominion and a granddaughter of the venerable ex–President of the late United States, had been elected to perform the principal part on this occasion. When the time arrived for raising the banner, Miss Tyler steadily and with heart throbbing with patriotic emotion, elevated it to the summit of the staff, cannon thundered forth a salute, the vast assemblage rent the air with shouts of welcome and the people of the South had for the first time a view of the Southern flag."

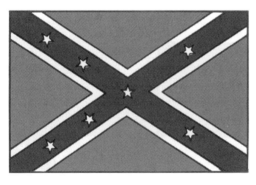

*Among the numerous other handsome designs rejected by the Confederate Congress in March of 1861 was this one submitted by Colonel Porcher Miles himself, chairman of the Flag Selection Committee. (One member of the committee laughed loudly at this design, saying that it looked like a pair of blue suspenders lying on a red tablecloth.) A year later, however, Miles would have better luck when this basic design was finally adopted. It would soon become known throughout the world as the Southern Cross, or the Battle Flag of the Confederacy. (Note that the above flag contains only seven stars, one for each state in the Confederacy in March of 1861.) (Cannon, Flags of the Confederacy)*

In April of 1861, a month following this celebration in Montgomery and just days following the firing on Fort Sumter, another presentation ceremony took place in New Orleans when a Miss Idelea Collens presented the colors to Louisiana's famous DeSoto Rifles with the following words:

"Receive then, from your mothers and sisters, from those whose affections greet you, these colors woven by our feeble but reliant hands; and when this bright flag shall float before you on the battlefield, let it not only inspire you with the brave and patriotic ambition of a soldier aspiring to his own and his country's honor and glory, but also may it be a sign that cherished ones appeal to you to save them from a fanatical and heartless foe."

Then the color sergeant took the flag from Miss Collens' hands and made another impassioned plea: "May the god of battles look down upon us as we register a soldier's vow that no stain shall ever be found upon thy sacred folds, save the blood of those who attack thee or those who fall in thy defense."

Interestingly enough, in 1911, a half century following these grand events of 1861, a controversy would erupt among the United Confederate Veterans as to just who should get credit for having designed the Stars and Bars. It was a distinction claimed by two Southern patriots, Orren R. Smith of North Carolina and Professor Nicola Marschall, a Prussia-born resident of Montgomery and a noted portrait artist. After much research and debate it was decided that though Professor Marschall's design had been close to the flag that was finally adopted, its dimensions were just a bit off the mark. And thus, decided the UCV, the distinction of having designed the Confederacy's celebrated Stars and Bars should go to Orren R. Smith.

## Major Orren R. Smith's Own Story

When the senators and representatives from the seven seceded states met at Montgomery, Alabama, in February of 1861, the first business after organizing was to decide whether the new nation should have a new flag and new constitution or fight under the Stars and Stripes and under the Constitution of the United States. Finally, a new constitution was adopted, and a committee was appointed to select a new flag. This committee advertised in the leading newspapers throughout the South for designs of flags to be sent to them at Montgomery. One of these advertisements went to Louisburg, N.C., where there was living a man, an original secessionist, who so hoped that the Confederacy would adopt a new flag and a new constitution that he was ready with a design when the "Flag Wanted" ad appeared.

Half a century later, in September 1910, when this man, Orren Randolph Smith, was introduced by General Julian S. Carr, commander of the United Confederate Veterans of North Carolina, at their reunion in Norfolk, Va., Major Smith told the following story:

"Three times have I been a soldier at my country's call, twice fighting under the Stars and Stripes and once under the Stars and Bars. While with Taylor, south of the Rio Grande, a unit in that proud army that never let an enemy touch our flag: in Utah with Albert Sidney Johnston, 1857–58, I learned what the flag meant to the men who were willing to give their lives for Old Glory every day and every hour in the day.

**Major Orren Smith,** *veteran of the Mexican War, the Indian wars, and the War Between the States, is credited with having designed the Stars and Bars. Here he is seen at the age of eighty, at a reunion of CSA veterans in 1910.* (Edwards and Broughton Printing Co., Raleigh, 1910)

A soldier's flag must be his inspiration. It stands for home, kindred and country; it must be something more than a piece of bunting or the blending of bright colors.

"When at Sumter, that shot was fired that was heard around the world, I realized that a new country had been made and that the new nation must have a new flag, of the deepest, truest significance, to lead the Men in Gray against the greatest odds and through the greatest difficulties that any soldiers have ever overcome since the world was made. The idea of my flag I took from the Trinity, Three in One. The three bars were for the Church, State and Press. Red represented the State, legislative, judiciary and executive; white for the Church, Father, Son and Holy Ghost; blue for press, freedom of speech, freedom of conscience and liberty of press— all bound together by a field of blue (the heavens over all), bearing a Star for each State in the Confederation. The seven white stars, all the same size, were placed in a circle, showing that each State had equal rights and privileges, irrespective of size or population. The circle, having neither head nor foot, stood for eternity, and signified You defend me and I'll protect you.

"I had the flag all complete in my mind before the Confederate Congress advertised for models, and when the advertisement appeared I went to my friend, Miss Rebecca Murphy (she is now Mrs. W. B. Winborne, of Wilson, N.C.), and asked if she would make me a little flag, I'd tell her how. I tore the Bars and she cut the Stars and she sewed the stitches, and when finished the little flag was sent to Montgomery, with the suggestion that a star be added for each State that joined the Confederacy. The flag committee, as you all know, accepted the flag and named it the Stars and Bars. They also adopted the suggestion, and it was not long before the flag bore eleven stars for the eleven Confederate States that voted for Jefferson Davis to be President.

"After the small flag was sent to Montgomery I bought dress goods from Barrow's store and asked Miss Rebecca to make me a large flag, 9 × 12 feet, for whether the flag committee accepted my model or not I was determined that one of my flags should be floating in the breeze. Splicing two tall saplings together, I made a pole one hundred feet high and planted it on the courthouse square at Louisburg, N.C. (where I was then living), and the flag was sent aloft on Monday, March 18, 1861, two months before North Carolina seceded. Over the flag was floating a long blue streamer, like an admiral has on his ship when "homeward bound," and on this pennant I had stars for each State that had seceded and one for North Carolina, for though my State was still in the Union I knew she was "homeward bound." This was the first Confederate flag ever raised in the Old North State, and this is how the Stars and Bars came into existence, "Dixie's Flag" that floated over the bravest and hardest to wear out soldiers ever encountered in any war."

Note: Miss Rebecca Murphy married first Dr. Germain Watson, and secondly W. B. Winborne. In 1904 Mrs. Winborne was living at Pine Top, N.C., and she appeared before W. L. Dunn, a justice of the peace and made an affidavit to having made the model flag for the Stars and Bars, and also for having made the large flag that flew over the courthouse in Louisburg. Major Orren R. Smith would later die at his home in Henderson, N.C.

**Flags of the Confederacy.** *Designed by Orren Randolph Smith of Louisburg, N.C., this is the original Stars and Bars, the first national flag of the Confederacy. It contained only seven stars.*

### The Birth of the Stars and Bars
*By Lelita Lever Younge,*
*(The Stonewall Jackson Chapter, No. 1135,*
*U.D.C., New Orleans, 1911)*
The shadow of a storm brooded o'er all,
The hearts of men were thrilled with sounds
 afar,
"What is this gloom that blackens like a pall?
If war must be," one cried, "then give us
 war!
Yet I have loved my country; I have cheered
The Stars and Stripes beneath the Mexic
 skies;
The bullet of the foe I have not feared!
All men are brothers — must we break such
 ties?"
War was declared. Fate rang Hope's funeral
 knell
The storm-cloud broke, and the Red, White
 and Blue
Flag he had bled for — he must bid farewell;
He ne'er had thought to recognize a new!
Inexorable decree! Southland so fair,
From Henceforth he was thine and thine
 alone —
Thine to the uttermost, to do and dare,
With soul determined, with the last doubt
 flown!
Home of the free, beloved and peerless land,
Thou had'st no flag to raise above the fray,
No emblem all thine own to lead thy band,
The brave, the true, the dauntless men in
 gray!
"A soldier's flag," he said with kindling
 glance,

"Must be his inspiration — something more
Than bunting and gay colors to enhance
Its meaning and significance." He bore
No bitterness within his lofty soul,
His great heart had no room for petty hate.
Right was his slogan, Freedom was his goal,
This Orren Randolph Smith! Whate'er the
 fate
Of the young Constitution, he would be
First to reveal its emblem to the world!
Thus musing, he selected symbols three —
Church, State and Press, on azure field
 unfurled.
Then seven stars he grouped in circle
 round — one
White star for each state — "For I know," he
 said,
"The Circle hath a meaning most profound,
Time and Eternity!" Blue, White and Red
He tore the bars and set them in their place,
And as with bated breath and rapture pure
The sire looks upon his first-born's face,
So he upon his Flag! What souls endure
In moments so supreme his soul endured!
Not even when he saw it in the dust,
To strife and blood and sorrow long inured,
Did he forsake the dear and holy trust.
Smith gave the South her Flag. The best in
 him
Was woven in its every sacred fold.
Though torn and tattered, faded, worn and
 dim,
Our hearts enshrine it still in Memory's gold.

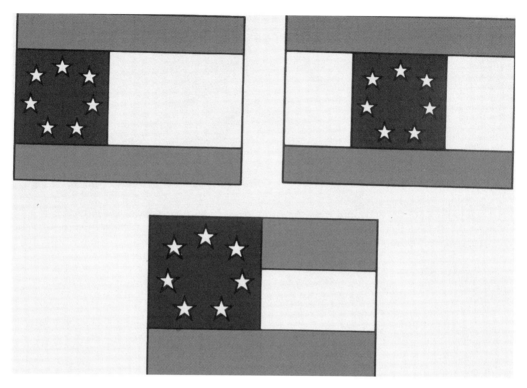

*Nicola Marschall submitted the three flags above to the Confederate Congress in March of 1861 for their consideration. Note that the first sample appears to be very similar to the flag finally chosen as the first national flag of the Confederacy, the Stars and Bars.*

*Professor Marschall was born in Prussia and settled in Mobile, Ala., where he became a noted artist and musician. Indeed, it was Prof. Marschall who painted the famous portrait of Nathan Bedford Forrest located on page 62. (Cannon,* Flags of the Confederacy*)*

**The Great Seal of the Confederacy** (The Museum of the Confederacy, Richmond)

*Top*: **South Carolina's Palmetto Flag** *flies from the Charleston Hotel in April 1861 as Governor Francis Pickens addresses the 35th Abbeville Volunteers.*
*Bottom*: *"Noli Me Tangere" warns the coiled snake on the flag of the Holcombe Legion. Lucy Holcombe Pickens, wife of Governor Pickens and the belle of the South, here reviews troops at Fort Moultrie in April 1861. (Lucy sold jewelry given to her by the czar of Russia to finance the raising of this company.)* (Photographs courtesy Frank and Marie-Theresse Wood Print Collections, Alexandria, Virginia)

Lucy Holcombe Pickens, *a native of Marshall, Texas, and the wife of South Carolina's Governor Francis Pickens. Noted for her beauty, she was called "The Queen of the Confederacy" and was the only female ever to have her likeness grace the face of Confederate currency.* (Civil War Times Illustrated)

A Confederate bill bearing the likeness of Lucy Pickens *is worth some $400 on today's market.* (Civil War Times Illustrated)

**Fort Sumter under fire,** *as seen here from the artillery batteries at Fort Moultrie, opening hostilities between the North and South in April of '61. This painting is by Conrad Chapman, the South's premier artist during the War Between the States.* (The Confederate Museum, Richmond Photo by Katherine Wetzel)

**The Trapier Mortar Battery on Morris Island in Charleston Harbor.** *It was from here that the first shots were fired on Fort Sumter.* (The Citadel Archives)

**Edmund Ruffin,** *seen here with his four children, was a Virginian and a rabid secessionist who was well known nationally for his experiments in agricultural chemistry. In 1860 his novel,* Anticipations of the Future, *predicted civil war and a Southern victory. Following Lee's surrender Ruffin committed suicide rather than live under Yankee rule.*

    *Depicted here (L–R): Julian Calx, Mildred Campbell, Charles Lorraine and Ella.* (Courtesy Mr. and Mrs. Sterling P. Anderson, Marlbourne, Va.)

**Opposite:** *This* **Frank Leslie print** *shows the women of Charleston watching the bombardment of Fort Sumter from rooftops located along the Battery. Not all are jubilant, however, and several appear to have their heads bowed in prayer.* (National Archives)

**The Stars and Bars** *flies triumphantly over Fort Sumter on April 15, 1861, after a bombardment forced Major Robert Anderson to withdraw his Union forces. (Note: Major Anderson promised southern negotiators that a lack of food and water would force his withdrawal from Fort Sumter by April 14 if they would only wait. We can only wonder how history might have been different if the South had waited instead of opening fire.)* (National Archives)

*Because of his outspoken States Rights views,* **Edmund Ruffin** *was given the honor of firing the first shot at Fort Sumter. This he did from an artillery piece on Morris Island. Here he is wearing the uniform and hat of South Carolina's Palmetto Guards.* (National Archives)

*Opposite:* **The Palmetto Artillery** *mans an emplacement on the Stono River, just south of Charleston, in April of 1861. Note that the standard bearer can hardly be more than fourteen years old.* (Library of Congress)

**Troops from South Carolina regiments** *inspect Fort Sumter on Monday, April 15, 1861, the day following Major Anderson's surrender.* (National Archives)

**Confederate officials inspect this 10-inch Columbiad at Fort Sumter.** *Wade Hampton is closest to the gun, wearing a top hat.* (National Archives)

# 2

# Generals

The seven full generals of the Confederate Army. Between 1861 and 1865 a total of 385 general officers served the Confederacy at one time or another, but there were only seven full generals.

*Samuel Cooper*

*Albert Sidney Johnston*

*Robert E. Lee*

*Joseph Johnston*

*P. G. T. Beauregard*

*Braxton Bragg*

*E. Kirby Smith*

**General Joseph Eggleston Johnston:** *An 1829 graduate of West Point and a classmate of Robert E. Lee, Johnston was the fourth highest ranking general in the Confederate Army. He and Jefferson Davis disliked one another intently, yet he resigned his position as quartermaster general of the U.S. Army to accept command of the Army of Virginia, which he commanded until terribly wounded at the Battle of Seven Pines on May 31, 1862. Three years later he surrendered his Army of Tennessee to General William T. Sherman in Greensboro, N.C. Following the war he served in the U.S. House of Representatives, and was appointed U.S. commissioner of railroads. He died in March of 1891 as the result of a cold contracted while serving as a pallbearer at the funeral of his old enemy, General William T. Sherman. (Someone offered Johnston an umbrella as protection against the sleet that was falling that frigid afternoon, but Johnston brushed it aside, saying, "Poor General Sherman, it's the least I can do for him. He would have done the same for me.")* (National Archives)

**The immortal Stonewall Jackson.** *Orphaned at the age of six, and with little formal education, Thomas J. Jackson graduated from West Point in 1846. (He was allowed to enter West Point only after a better qualified boy from his hometown refused his appointment.) He is still reputed to be one of the most industrious students ever to enroll at that institution, and one of the most brilliant field generals ever to command an army. His death in 1863 was a devastating blow to the Confederacy.* (National Archives)

**General P. G. T. Beauregard** (1818–1893): *An 1838 graduate of West Point, he accepted the surrender of Fort Sumter from Colonel Robert Anderson. He had enjoyed an outstanding military career prior to the war and was famous for his engineering skills. He commanded Confederate forces at the First Manassas, even though he was outranked by General Joseph Johnston, and was promoted to full generalship the day following that battle. But Beauregard was constantly feuding with Jefferson Davis and his fellow generals, and thus in January '62 he was ordered west and placed under General Albert Sidney Johnston. Following Johnston's death at Pittsburg Landing in September of '62, command in the west went to General Braxton Bragg, and Beauregard was ordered to take command of forces in South Carolina and Georgia. Following the war he enjoyed a very lucrative engineering position in New Orleans. Later, in 1893, he and Jubal Early became supervisors of the infamous Louisiana lottery. While a professor at West Point during the 1830s, Robert Anderson stated that Cadet Beauregard was the finest student he'd ever taught.* (National Archives)

*Jackson upon his graduation from West Point in 1846.* (National Archives)

*In 1848 Jackson distinguished himself as a lieutenant of artillery with Winfield Scott in Mexico.* (The Lexington Foundation's Stonewall Jackson House)

*Jackson in 1855 as a Virginia Military Institute professor of natural science.* (National Archives)

**General Bernard Bee** (1824–1861): *A South Carolinian yelled, "There stands Jackson like a stone wall. Rally around the Virginians"* at the First Manassas. *Bee was the highest ranking officer killed in that great battle.* (National Archives)

*In August of 1853 Jackson, by then a VMI professor, married Eleanor Junkin who died in 1854.*
*Then in July of '57 he married Anna Morrison, daughter of the president of Davidson College.*
*General D. H. Hill, a math professor at Davidson, was married to Anna's sister and was one of*
*Jackson's dearest friends. Here Jackson and Anna are pictured with their daughter Julia, known*
*as Little Miss Stonewall.* (Stonewall Jackson House Collection, Historic Lexington Foundation)

*In this somewhat fanciful portrait of Jackson, a devout Presbyterian, his hand is resting appropriately on the Bible.* (By William Sartain, Anne Brown Military Collection, Brown University)

**Julia "Little Miss Stonewall" Jackson,** 1880. (Stonewall Jackson House Collection, Historic Lexington Foundation)

**Anna Morrison Jackson,** 1880. (Stonewall Jackson House Collection, Historic Lexington Foundation)

**General Albert Sidney Johnston** (1803–1862): *An 1826 graduate of West Point and a classmate of Jefferson Davis, Johnston was outranked in the CSA by only General Samuel Cooper (then came Lee, Joe Johnston, Beauregard and Bragg). Because of his brilliant military career, he was appointed a full general in 1861 and placed in command of all Confederate forces in the Western Theater. During his heroic fight at Shiloh in April of '62, he bled to death from a minor leg wound before help could arrive. His death proved a devastating blow to the Confederacy.* (National Archives)

*This handsome bust of General Albert Sidney Johnston is on display in the Valentine Museum in Richmond.* (The Valentine Museum)

**General Edmund Kirby Smith** (1824–1893): *Born in St. Augustine, Florida, Smith was the son of a federal judge and was an 1845 graduate of West Point. In 1861 he was assigned to Harpers Ferry as adjutant to General Joe Johnston. Following the First Manassas, he was promoted to brigadier general and named commander of forces in East Tennessee. Following the standoff at Chaplin Hills in October of '62, Smith decided to resign his commission and become a minister. But after a sudden promotion to lieutenant general and command of forces in the Trans-Mississippi theater, Smith changed his mind. In February of '64 he was appointed a full general. During the final year of the war he moved his headquarters to Houston, Texas, with intentions of continuing the war from that great state if possible. He surrendered his army on June 2, 1865, some six weeks after the surrender of General Lee. From 1865–67 he headed the Atlantic and Pacific Telegraph Co. in Nashville, and later became president of the University of Nashville.* (National Archives)

**Lieutenant General William J. Hardee** (1815–1872): *An 1838 graduate of West Point, Hardee authored a famous textbook on military tactics that was used by both the Confederacy and the Union throughout the war. He was called to Montgomery in '61 to help organize the Confederate Army, and was promoted to lieutenant general following the battle of Pittsburgh Landing. He served as a corps commander in Braxton Bragg's Army of Tennessee, and following the South's defeat at Chaplin Hills, he urged Jefferson Davis to replace Bragg immediately, an event that did nothing to enhance Bragg's reputation in Richmond. In July of '64 his army was nearly destroyed at Atlanta. Following the war he served as president of the Selma and Meridian Railroad.* (National Archives)

**General Robert E. Lee** (Library of Congress)

**General Robert E. Lee** *assumed command of the Army of Northern Virginia on June 1, 1862, following the wounding of General Joe Johnston at the Battle of Seven Pines. (This photograph was taken on the back porch of Lee's home in Richmond only hours after his surrender to General Grant.)* (National Archives)

*An 1829 graduate of West Point, this is Lieutenant Robert E. Lee in 1838.* (Washington and Lee University)

**Mary Anna Custis,** *the granddaughter of George and Martha Washington, at the time of her wedding to Robert E. Lee in 1831.* (Washington & Lee University)

*Lee and son Rooney in a photo taken at Fort Hamilton, New York, in 1842.* (Virginia Historical Society)

**Robert E. Lee** *graduated second in his class at West Point to Charles Mason (above). Mason served only a brief enlistment in the army before resigning to become an attorney and a judge.* (Charles Mason Remey, Chicago Historical Society)

**Colonel Robert E. Lee** *in 1851 while overseeing the construction of Fort Carroll in Maryland.* (Library of Congress)

**Major General Gustavus W. Smith** (1821–96): *An 1842 graduate of West Point and the former street commissioner of New York City, Smith was considered a fine catch for the Confederacy in 1861. But in time he proved to be a most eccentric gentleman who suffered from psychosomatic bouts of paralysis. In May of 1862, following Joe Johnston's wounding at Seven Pines, Jeff Davis offered Smith command of the Army of Northern Virginia, but Smith was forced to decline, claiming that he was suffering a bout of paralysis. Command of the army was then offered to General Robert E. Lee. In 1864–65 Smith distinguished himself as he led the Georgia militia in a spirited defense of Atlanta and Savannah.* (Valentine Museum)

*Lee served as superintendent of West Point from 1852 until 1855. John B. Hood, Fitzhugh Lee, John Pegram, O. O. Howard, J. E. B. Stuart and Phil Sheridan were cadets during Lee's tenure at the military academy.* (Frick Art Reference Library, New York)

**Mary Custis Lee,** *the Lees' oldest daughter, remained a spinster and spent much of her adult life touring the great capitals of Europe as the honored guest of numerous kings and queens.* (Mrs. Hunter deButts Collection)

**George Washington Custis "Boo" Lee** *was the Lees' oldest son. He graduated first in his class at West Point in 1854, served as a general in the war and in 1872 succeeded his father as president of Washington & Lee College (1872–97).* (Washington & Lee University)

**Major General W. H. F. "Rooney" Lee** (1837–1891), *the Lees' second son, was a Harvard graduate, and served with distinction as commander of the Ninth Virginia Cavalry at Fredericksburg. Later, he was wounded and taken prisoner at Brandy Station. Once paroled, he served with Stuart's Cavalry for the duration. He returned home at war's end to find his property destroyed and his wife and two children dead. He would serve as a congressman from Virginia from 1886 until his death in 1891.* (Library of Congress)

**Robert E. "Rob" Lee, Jr.,** *the Lees' youngest son, a graduate of the University of Virginia, joined the army as a private and eventually rose to the rank of captain. It is said that General Lee twice met his son on the field of battle but failed to recognize him on either occasion because the younger Lee was so covered in dirt and grime.* (Library of Congress)

**Agnes Lee,** *the Lees' middle daughter. The Yan-kees hanged her fiancé, Colonel Orton Williams, as a spy. It was a shock from which she never fully recovered.* (Mrs. Hunter deButts Collection)

**Mildred Lee,** *the Lees' youngest daughter, never married. Comparing other men with her father, she said, "To me he seems a hero, all other men small in comparison."* (Mrs. Hunter deButts Collection)

*This Brady photo, taken on April 16, 1865, depicts* **General Custis Lee, General Lee,** *and Lee's aide (and later biographer),* **Colonel Walter Taylor.** (Library of Congress)

**Lee's three sons in later life** *(L–R): Robert E. "Rob" Lee, Jr., George Washington Custis Lee, and Rooney Lee.* (Virginia Historical Society)

**General Robert E. Lee's Headquarters Flag.** (The Museum of the Confederacy, Richmond. Photograph by Katherine Wetzel)

**Lieutenant General James Longstreet** (1821–1904): *An 1842 graduate of West Point, Longstreet commanded Lee's First Corps throughout the war. Indeed, it was said that "in combat he had few equals." At Gettysburg Longstreet strongly urged Lee to fight a defensive battle but to no avail. Earlier in his career, while serving the Missouri frontier, he served as best man when his first cousin married his dearest friend, Lieutenant Ulysses S. Grant. Following the war President Grant appointed him ambassador to Turkey. (He was the nephew of famed novelist Augustus Baldwin Longstreet.)* (Cook Collection, Valentine Museum)

**Lieutenant General Richard Stoddard Ewell** (1817–72): *An 1840 graduate of West Point and a career military man. Despite having had his left leg shot away at Second Manassas in 1862, Ewell was given command of Lee's Second Corps following the death of Stonewall Jackson in 1863, and it was Ewell who led the drive into Gettysburg. A nervous, fidgety man, he suffered from a severe speech impediment and was famous among his fellow generals for his hot temper and rich use of profanity. Indeed, on his way to Gettysburg he paused long enough at Winchester to demand the surrender of Union commander General Robert Milroy, informing him that he was surrounded by a superior force. Milroy responded that should Ewell attack, he would "put the torch to the city." Ewell replied, "You do, and I'll put the bayonet to your ass." Following the war he and his wife, Lizinka Ewell, retired to Spring Hill, Tennessee, where Lizinka owned a large plantation.* (Cook Collection, Valentine Museum)

*In this Frances Gutekunst work, entitled "Jefferson Davis and His Confederate Generals," it is interesting to note that grouped around Davis are his favorite generals (A. P. Hill, John Bell Hood, J. E. B. Stuart, Stonewall Jackson and Robert E. Lee). Separated somewhat from this group are those less favored (James Longstreet, Joseph E. Johnston, P. G. T. Beauregard, and Jubal Early.)* (The Naval Historical Center, Washington, D.C.)

**Lieutenant General Ambrose Powell Hill** (1825–65): *An 1847 graduate of West Point, A. P. Hill is remembered as one of the South's finest generals. Both Jackson and Longstreet were constantly at odds with Hill and both had him arrested for insubordination. Still, he is credited with having preserved a Southern victory at Sharpsburg, and later he commanded Lee's Third Corps at Gettysburg. Indeed, General Mahone said of him, "A more brilliant, useful soldier and chivalrous gentleman never adorned the Confederate Army." Early in his career Hill's fiancée, Nelly Marcy, broke off their engagement that she might marry Captain George McClellan, Hill's roommate at West Point. Later he would marry Kitty Morgan, sister of Colonel John Hunt Morgan, and they would have four daughters. Oddly enough, the last words of both Jackson and Lee, delirious during their dying moments, concerned A. P. Hill. Jackson, with his last breath, gasped, "Tell A.P. Hill he must come up on my left flank immediately." And Lee, who died*

*nine years later, roused up just long enough to say, "Please tell General Hill he must try to come up as quickly as possible." Hill was killed during the final defense of Petersburg on April 2, 1865.* (National Archives)

**Brigadier General Maxcy Gregg** (1814–62): *A South Carolinian with no prior military training, he served in the South Carolina Secession Convention, then became a colonel with the First South Carolina Infantry. He was noted for his courage and became one of Stonewall Jackson's most trusted lieutenants. He was mortally wounded at Fredericksburg in December of 1862. When Jackson learned that Gregg was dying, he went immediately to his bedside, and, ignoring his own exhaustion, spent the whole long night holding Gregg's hand, praying and trying to comfort his doomed friend in every way possible. The noble Gregg finally died at dawn.* (The South Caroliniana Library, University of South Carolina)

**Major General John Bankhead Magruder** (1807–71): *A West Point graduate and a veteran of the Mexican War, he defended the lower Virginia peninsula during much of the war. His fondness for high society and gaudy uniforms earned him the nickname Prince John. He also had a speech impediment which led one Richmond lady to say, "He lisps and swears at the same time." Following the war he fled to Mexico and served in the army of Maximilan. In 1871 he died in Houston, Texas.* (Library of Congress)

**Brigadier General Turner Ashby** (1828–1862): *A native of Faquier County, Va., he came under the command of Stonewall Jackson at Harpers Ferry in 1861, and was assigned to take his company of Virginia militia and guard river crossings all the way to Point of Rocks, Md. Ashby soon became indispensable to Jackson and was named colonel of the Seventh Virginia Cavalry. By March of '62, following a series of outstanding performances, Jackson promoted Ashby to brigadier general. He was killed by a bullet to the heart while covering Jackson's retreat from Harrisonburg. Though he lacked military skill, his scouting abilities and reckless daring earned him the name "White Knight of the Valley."* (Library of Congress)

*A snappy little ditty published in 1862 extolling the exploits of General Turner Ashby.* (Library of Congress)

**The 18th Mississippi Infantry** *defended the Sunken Lane at Fredericksburg in December of '62, and is credited with stopping Burnside's charge at Marye's Heights despite suffering horrendous casualties.* (National Archives, Civil War #96)

**General Braxton Bragg** (1817–1876): *An 1837 graduate of West Point and the fifth ranking officer in the Confederate Army, Bragg was given command of the Army of Tennessee following the death of General Albert Sidney Johnston. A brilliant leader, he suffered terribly from chronic migraine headaches, a condition which doubtlessly affected his relationships with his subordinates and his effectiveness in the field. In December of '62, following much criticism of his performances to date, he requested that he be relieved of his command, and thus Jefferson Davis transferred him to Richmond to serve as a military advisor to the president.* (Cook Collection, Valentine Museum)

**Brigadier General Simon Bolivar Buckner** (1823–1914): *An 1844 graduate of West Point, Buckner served in the Mexican War, then became an instructor at West Point until 1855. In 1860 he was placed in command of the Kentucky State Militia, and occupied Bowling Green when war broke out in '61. Later, on February 16, 1862, surrounded by Grant's forces at Fort Donelson, he and his command remained behind while John B. Floyd, Gideon Pillow, and Nathan Bedford Forrest made their escape. Following a prisoner exchange, he was promoted to major general and placed in command of a division in Hardee's army. He was praised highly for his performance at Chaplin Hills on October 8, 1862, and in September of '63 he commanded a corps at Chickamauga under General Longstreet. Following that great victory, Buckner, along with several other generals, signed a petition demanding General Bragg's removal from the Army of Tennessee. In April of '64 he was assigned to General Kirby Smith's Western Army and placed in command of western Louisiana, Mississippi and Tennessee. Following the war Buckner was elected governor of Kentucky.*

Following Buckner's surrender to General Grant at Fort Donelson, he received a note from Grant which read, "You are far from home and friends. Perhaps you need funds. My purse is open to you." In a snit because his old friend would only agree to an unconditional surrender, Buckner snubbed both Grant and his offer of a loan. He was later elected governor of Kentucky, and served as a pallbearer at Grant's funeral. (Library of Congress)

**Lieutenant General Nathan Bedford Forrest** (1821–1877): *In 1861 Forrest, along with his 15-year-old son, volunteered as a private in the Seventh Tennessee Cavalry, but was soon authorized to raise a company of cavalry (the Third Tennessee Cavalry) with himself as colonel. In February of '62, following his successful escape from Union forces at Fort Donelson, he was promoted to brigadier general and placed in command of Forrest's Cavalry Brigade. In December of '62 he so disrupted Union supply lines that Grant had to postpone his attack at Vicksburg. He later played a vital role in Bragg's victory over Rosecrans at Chickamauga. When Bragg failed to pursue fleeing Union forces following that great battle, the rambunctious Forrest assailed him with: "If you were half a man I'd slap your damned head off." Instead of a court-martial, Forrest was rewarded with his own independent command and sent to Mississippi. Sherman called Forrest "the most remarkable man our Civil War produced on either side." Truly, in the opinion of many, Forrest was the foremost cavalry leader of the entire war. Returned to civilian life, he worked as president of a railroad.* (Nicola Marschall. Library of Congress)

**Major General Earl Van Dorn** (1820–1863): *An 1842 graduate of West Point, Van Dorn was the great-nephew of Andrew Jackson and the recipient of one of the three Battle Flags made by the Cary girls. He served in the Trans-Mississippi theater, and is best remembered for the loss he suffered at Elkhorn Tavern. He served as a commander of cavalry in Bragg's Army of Tennessee, and in '62 was placed in command of cavalry at Vicksburg under General John Pemberton. He was assassinated by a jealous husband in May of '63. (It was said that Van Dorn and John Bell Hood were actively pursued by every young belle in Richmond.)* (Library of Congress)

*The battle flag carried by Van Dorn's Army of the Mississippi. This particular flag was the battle flag of the 4th Mississipppi Infantry Regiment.* (The Confederate Museum, Richmond. Photograph by Katherine Wetzel)

**Major General John C. Breckinridge** (1821–75): *Breckinridge was from one of Kentucky's most prominent families and educated at Centre College, Princeton, and Transylvania University. Later, following a term in the U.S. Senate, he served as vice president under James Buchanan. In 1862 his brigade performed so well at Pittsburgh Landing that he was promoted to major general in the Army of Tennessee under General Braxton Bragg. His division suffered such heavy casualties at Murfreesboro that Breckinridge threatened to shoot Bragg, whom he blamed for the debacle. On November 25, at Missionary Ridge his corps was overrun by a superior Union force, and General Bragg eagerly removed him from command. But General Lee stepped in and placed Breckinridge in command of southwestern Virginia. There on May 15, 1864, with the support of the cadets from VMI, he defeated a larger force at New Market. In February of '65, President Davis appointed him secretary of war. With General Lee's surrender, Breckinridge fled to Canada, where he remained until 1868. He then returned to Lexington where he practiced law until his death in 1875.* (The South Caroliniana Library, University of South Carolina)

"The Last Meeting" *(by E. B. F. Julio) captures a dawn meeting between Robert E. Lee and Stonewall Jackson at Chancellorsville on May 2, 1863. Late that evening Jackson would receive the wounds that would lead to his death shortly thereafter. Here Lee is depicted upon his favorite horse, Traveler, while Jackson is astride Little Sorrel.* (Anne Brown Military Collection, Brown University)

**Lieutenant General Jubal Anderson Early** (1816–1894): *An 1837 graduate of West Point, Early wreaked havoc against the Federals in the Shenandoah following Jackson's death in 1863. He was highly critical of his southern colleagues and had an irascible nature, leading General Lee to jokingly refer to him as "my bad old man." Indeed, at Lynchburg Early delighted his troops when he stood in his saddle and shouted at retreating Union cavalry, "No buttermilk rangers after you now, you goddamned blue-butted bastards."* (Valentine Museum)

*A dedicated Unionist prior to the war, Old Jube eventually became the most unreconstructed of all southern leaders. At war's end, disguised as a farmer, he escaped to Mexico rather than live under Yankee rule. In 1869 he returned to the United States.* (Valentine Museum)

**Major General George Pickett** (1825–1875): *An 1846 graduate of West Point, Pickett early in the war distinguished himself at the Seven Days' and Seven Pines battles, and was then placed in command of General Longstreet's First Corps. Certainly no other action of the war is remembered like Pickett's ill-fated charge at Gettysburg on July 3, 1863. Rarely has the world seen such courage and heroism as was displayed by the southern boys in that engagement. Following the war he became an insurance executive in Norfolk, Va.*

*When Pickett became a father during the fighting around Petersburg, his old West Point friend, General Ulysses S. Grant, had bonfires lighted in his honor. As though that were not enough, Grant then sent a very expensive silver service to Pickett for his wife LaSalle Pickett.* (Library of Congress)

**General George Pickett and his lovely young wife, LaSalle Corbell Pickett.** *At the time of their marriage in 1863 Corbell was fifteen, Pickett thirty-eight. (This was his third marriage.) She bore him two children, one son, George Pickett, Jr., and a daughter, Corbell. Following Pickett's death in 1875, Corbell fought valiantly for the rest of her life to defend his reputation against all detractors. She survived her husband by 56 years, dying in 1931.*

*In 1998, one hundred and twenty-three years following General Pickett's death, Corbell's remains were disinterred and placed next to her husband's in Richmond's Hollywood Cemetery.* (Mrs. Billie B. Ernest)

**Brigadier General Lewis Armistead** (1817–1863): *Killed at Gettysburg, he was called "without peer" as a brigade commander in Lee's Army of Northern Virginia. As a freshman cadet at West Point in 1836, Armistead was expelled for breaking a heavy dinner plate over the head of senior cadet Jubal Early who had been teasing the shy Armistead about a young lady friend. In 1848, after distinguishing himself for bravery during the war with Mexico, he was promoted to major. In later years, while he and Winfield Scott Hancock served together on the western frontier, Hancock became his dearest friend, and Armistead received permission from General Lee to meet with Hancock (now a Union general) at Gettysburg under a flag of truce. Armistead, unfortunately, was killed before that meeting could take place. As he lay dying in a Union hospital on July 5, he requested that his watch and other valuables be sent to General Hancock.*

*Only moments prior to his fatal charge at Gettysburg, General Armistead removed a gold ring from his finger and handed it to General Pickett, requesting that he send it to his lovely wife LaSalle as a memento "from one who envies her lucky husband."* (Library of Congress)

**Brigadier General Porter Alexander** (1835–1910): *An 1837 graduate of West Point, Alexander remained at the academy for another four years as an instructor of engineering. In 1861 he joined the Confederacy and General Beauregard named him chief of the Signal Corps. He constructed an observation tower at Manassas, and it was said that the intelligence he gathered on Union troop movements on July 20–21 was largely responsible for the Confederacy's great win. Later in '61 he was named chief of ordnance for both Beauregard and Joe Johnston. In the summer of '62 General Robert E. Lee, highly impressed with Alexander's performances, gave him command of General Stephen D. Lee's artillery battalion. Later he was named chief of artillery for Lee's First Corps. It was said that his guns were essential to Southern victories at both Fredericksburg and Chancellorsville. Indeed, it was Alexander's artillery that shelled Union positions just prior to Pickett's charge at Gettysburg, and it was his artillery that doomed Union efforts at Cold Harbor on June 3, 1864. Following the war he served as president of a railroad and as a professor of engineering.* (National Archives)

**Major General Isaac Trimble** (1802–1888): *He graduated from West Point in 1822 and became the most prominent soldier from Maryland to serve in the Confederate Army. As commander of the Baltimore defenses, in 1861 Trimble disrupted the passage of Union troops into that city. Then he was placed in command of a division in Ewell's Second Corps. He served valiantly in Jackson's Shenandoah and Seven Days campaigns. At Gettysburg, while leading two North Carolina brigades in the Pickett-Pettigrew charge, he was severely wounded and taken prisoner. He was not released until war's end.* (Library of Congress)

**Major General Edward Johnson** (1816–1873): *He graduated from West Point in 1838 and served in the U.S. Army until 1861. In 1862 he was placed in command of the Stonewall Division in Lee's Army of Northern Virginia, and distinguished himself as a member of Ewell's Second Corps at Gettysburg. The following year he was captured at Spotsylvania, exchanged five months later, and placed in charge of a division in the Army of Tennessee. In December of '64 he was again captured at Nashville and remained a prisoner until war's end.* (National Archives)

**Major General John B. Gordon** (1832–1904): *In 1861 Gordon and his Georgia volunteers arrived in Virginia just in time to occupy General Beauregard's right flank at First Manassas on July 21. At Seven Pines Gordon took command of General Rodes' brigade when that officer went down with a wound. He was in the thick of the fight at Sharpsburg where he was wounded five times. Assigned to Jubal Early, Gordon's brigade led attacks at both Chancellorsville and Gettysburg. In the final days, Gordon's troops attacked Fort Stedman in hopes of allowing General Lee's main army to escape to North Carolina. Following the war Gordon was twice elected to the U.S. Senate and in 1886 was elected governor of Georgia.* (National Archives)

**Major General Robert Emmett Rodes** (1829–64): *An 1849 graduate of VMI, Rodes worked as an engineer in Alabama until 1861. Promoted to brigadier general in October of that year, he fought with distinction at Seven Pines until he received a serious head wound. Several weeks later he rejoined Lee's army in Maryland, and his brigade desperately defended the Bloody Lane at Sharpsburg. Later his division played a key role at Fredericksburg during Stonewall Jackson's famous flank attack. In 1863 it was Rodes' division that first attacked Union positions at Gettysburg on July 1. Fighting with Jubal Early in the Valley in '64, Rodes was killed on September 19, 1864, at Winchester. He has always been remembered as one of General Lee's most trusted officers.* (Library of Congress)

*Left:* Major General Fitzhugh Lee (1835–1905): *A West Point graduate in 1856, Fitzhugh Lee was the nephew of General Robert E. Lee, and fought valiantly with Stuart's Cavalry throughout the war. In '63 he became the South's youngest major general. Following the war he served as governor of Virginia and later, during the war with Spain, became a general in the U.S. Army and military governor of Cuba. As a freshman at West Point he suffered the ignominy of being court-martialed by his uncle for being absent from the barracks without permission.* (Library of Congress)

*Right:* Major General Thomas Rosser (1836–1910): *He resigned from West Point when Texas seceded in '61, and was given command of the Fifth Virginia Cavalry. In '64 he distinguished himself for daring while serving with Jubal Early in the Shenandoah. His roommate and best friend at West Point had been George Armstrong Custer, with whom he served on the western frontier following the war. In 1898 he became a general in the U.S. Army.* (Library of Congress)

*Left:* Major General Robert F. Hoke (1837–1912): *A North Carolinian, Hoke entered the army as a private in 1861 but was promoted to brigadier general following an outstanding performance under Jubal Early at Fredericksburg. Wounded at Chancellorsville, Hoke was transferred to North Carolina in '63, where he captured the strongly fortified town of Plymouth (called one of the most brilliant victories of the war, and for which he was promoted to major general). He finally surrendered with Joe Johnston at Bentonville, N.C., in 1865.* (Library of Congress)

**Lieutenant General John C. Pemberton** (1814–1888): *An 1837 graduate of West Point, a career military officer and a native of Philadelphia who married a lady from Virginia, Pemberton came South in '61 and was given command of Confederate forces in South Carolina and Georgia. He alarmed and angered Carolinians (and President Davis) when he stated that he would abandon Charleston rather than risk losing his army to an invading force. Davis then promoted him to lieutenant general and placed him in command of forces in East Louisiana, including Vicksburg, possibly the most difficult assignment in the South. After turning back Grant's attempts to take Vicksburg in the winter of '62 and '63, he received a series of conflicting orders from his commander, Joe Johnston, and President Davis. Davis warned him not to leave the city under any circumstances, while Johnston ordered him to leave and attack Grant. Pemberton obeyed Davis, and on July 4, following a 47-day siege, he surrendered the city. Johnston thus blamed Pemberton for the defeat because he had disobeyed his orders to attack. Pemberton requested a reduction in rank, and thus spent the remainder of the war as colonel of artillery in Virginia and South Carolina. Following the war he lived in both Philadelphia and Virginia.* (National Archives)

**Lieutenant General D. H. Hill** (1825–80): *An 1842 graduate of West Point, Hill distinguished himself as an officer in the Mexican War, then served as a Davidson College math professor until 1861. He soon became one of Lee's favorite generals, though he was heartily disliked by both Jefferson Davis and Braxton Bragg, which did his military career little good. Following the war he authored an algebra textbook that was adopted by universities across America, and later became president of the University of Arkansas. (He was the brother-in-law of Stonewall Jackson.)* (National Archives)

**Major General Dabney H. Maury** (1827–1900): *An 1846 graduate of West Point and a classmate of Stonewall Jackson, Maury became a career military officer who later taught at West Point (his open support of secession resulted in his dismissal in 1861). Assigned to Van Dorn's Trans-Mississippi Department, his cavalry fought at Elkhorn Tavern as well as Iuka and Corinth. In December of '62 his unit was sent to reinforce Stephen Dill Lee's force at Vicksburg. Then in April he reported to Knoxville as commander of the Army of East Tennessee. Soon thereafter he was moved to Mobile as commander of the District of the Gulf. For the next two years he used his intelligence and ingenuity to keep Mobile and Mobile Bay free of Federal invaders, and did not surrender Mobile until April of '65. Following the war he was named ambassador to Colombia. He is also credited with having founded the Southern Historical Society.* (The Civil War Times Illustrated)

The Headquarters Flag of General Dabney H. Maury. (Museum of the Confederacy)

**Major General James Ewell Brown Stuart**
(1834–1864): *An 1854 graduate of West Point who personified the cavalier spirit of the entire Confederate Army. When told that his father-in-law, General Philip St. George Cook (for whom Stuart had named his son) had refused to resign his commission in the Federal cavalry, Stuart said, "He will regret it but once, and that will be continuously." He then had his son's name legally changed to James Ewell Brown. Called a "master" of cavalry tactics, Stuart played an essential role in General Lee's successes in northern Virginia. On June 12, 1862, he became famous for his incredible three-day ride around McClellan's entire army. He was mortally wounded at Yellow Tavern in 1864 when he was but 29 years old. His last request as he lay dying at his brother-in-law's home in Richmond was for someone to sing "Rock of Ages," his favorite song.* (The Naval Historical Center, Washington, D.C.)

**Stephen Dill Lee, Jeb Stuart, and George Washington Custis Lee** *in a photograph made immediately following their graduation from West Point in 1854. Stephen Dill Lee was an outstanding South Carolinian who fought bravely from Fort Sumter to Bentonville. Custis "Boo" Lee was the oldest son of General Lee and spent the war on the staff of Jefferson Davis. As for the illustrious J. E. B. Stuart, he was twice expelled from West Point for insubordination, but on both occasions was immediately reinstated because of his "extreme youth." (Stuart was known to his classmates as "Beauty" because of his undisciplined and combative nature.)* (The Virginia Historical Society)

**Laura Ratcliffe:** *A real Southern beauty at the age of 25. Early in the war Laura nursed the wounded of Stuart's Cavalry and it was rumored that Stuart was deeply in love with her, a rumor which he denied in a letter to his wife, Flora. Still, it is known that he carried a lock of her hair in his hatband and that upon her death at the age of 87 in 1923 there was found among her personal effects Stuart's gold watch chain and several affectionate letters and poems (see below).* (Virginia State Library)

### To Laura
J. E. B. Stuart, March 3, 1862*

*We met by chance: yet in that 'ventful chance*
*The mystic web of destiny was woven:*
*I saw thy beauteous image bend o'er*
*The prostrate form of one that day had proven*
*A hero fully nerved to deal*
*To tyrant hordes — the south's avenging steel.*
*'Twas woman's cherished sphere.*
*Thy self devotion —*
*Enchained my heart: were all as true as thou,*
*This war were not, and peace were still our*
*  portion.*
*I saw thee soothe the soldier's aching brow —*
*And ardent wished his lot were mine —*
*To be caressed with care like thine.*
*Fair Laura, (I flatter not) — thy praise*
*Is writ in words which war's alarms*
*Or time can ne'er from mem'ry efface*
*Thy worth, thy modesty, not the least of*
*  charms —*

*Will be the soul-inspiring theme*
*To fill the enraptured "soldier's dream."*
*The past to one is precious; and to thee —*
*I trust it is not all regret, be even*
*In war's dread desolation there may be*
*Some charmed remembrance to its havoc given*
*Some long-cherished, ne'er forgotten token*
*One friendship made ne'er to be broken.*
*To Him omnipotent I leave thee now —*
*Years, long years, our paths, may sever*
*May grief o'er shadow ne'er my Laura's*
*  brow —*
*And fortune smile upon thee ever.*
*And when this page shall meet your glance*
*Forget not him, you met by chance.*

*The above poem, written by J. E. B. Stuart in 1862, was found among Laura Ratcliffe's personal effects upon her death in 1923, some 61 years after the fact.

**Brigadier General Joseph Kershaw** (1822–94): *A native of Camden, South Carolina, Kershaw commanded the DeKalb Rifle Guards in the Mexican War and in February of '61 became a member of the Charleston Secession Convention. Following the firing on Fort Sumter he would lead the Second South Carolina Infantry, a regiment heavily engaged in the fighting throughout the war. In September of '63, his troops crushed the Union right flank at Chickamauga. And he was with Micah Jenkins when Jenkins was killed at the Wilderness in May of '64. Following the war he became active in state politics, and finally, in 1893, was appointed postmaster of Camden.* (The South Caroliniana Library, University of South Carolina)

**Sergeant William Smith's** *flag had been pierced by 74 Yankee bullets before the battle had ended. He later served in the U.S. Army during the Spanish-American War.* (The Virginia Historical Society)

*Holding aloft his tattered battle flag is Sergeant William Smith of the 12th Virginia Infantry as Confederate forces under General William Mahone successfully counterattack at the Battle of the Crater on July 30, 1864.* (Library of Congress)

**Major General William Mahone** *(1826–1895): An 1847 graduate of VMI, Mahone worked as a railroad engineer prior to the war. In 1861 he commanded the Sixth Virginia Infantry and performed brilliantly at both Malvern Hill and the Second Manassas. He is best remembered for routing Union troops at the Battle of the Crater. Following the war he returned to railroading, and was elected to the U.S. Senate in 1880. Mahone, who stood 5'4" and weighed 110 pounds, was affectionately known to his troops as Little Billy.* (National Archives)

**Lieutenant General Wade Hampton:** *One of the wealthiest plantation owners in the South, Hampton organized the Hampton Legion in '61. Assigned to Stuart's cavalry, the legion participated in some of the bloodiest battles of the war, and Hampton became commander of Lee's cavalry following Jeb Stuart's death in 1864. His son, Preston, was killed at Petersburg that same year. Because Hampton hanged Yankees guilty of crimes against southern civilians, Sherman refused to shake his hand when accepting Joe Johnston's surrender in 1865. In 1878 it was Hampton and his Red Shirts who unceremoniously drove the Carpetbaggers from South Carolina. He later served as governor of that great state.* (South Caroliniana Library, University of South Carolina)

**Colonel Frank Hampton:** *The younger brother of Wade Hampton, he was killed at Fredericksburg. His wife, a native of New York, was the former fiancée of famed British author Charles Dickens. (She broke off her engagement to the struggling Dickens and married the prosperous Hampton after her father suffered severe financial reverses.)* (South Caroliniana Library, University of South Carolina)

**Lieutenant General Stephen Dill Lee** (1833–1908): *A native of Charleston and an 1854 graduate of West Point, Lee served as aide-de-camp to General Beauregard while negotiating the surrender of Fort Sumter. Early in the war he was in the forefront of the fighting in northern Virginia, and was promoted to lieutenant general at the age of thirty, the youngest lieutenant general in either army. He was appointed a corps commander late in the conflict and assigned to the Army of Tennessee under General Joe Johnston, and was with Johnston when the final surrender came at Bentonville, N.C. He would later serve as the first president of Mississippi A&M College (Mississippi State University), and was the founder of the United Confederate Veterans. It was said that Lee was the only Confederate general officer both liked and respected by Nathan Bedford Forrest, quite a compliment.* (South Caroliniana Library, University of South Carolina)

**Lieutenant General John Bell Hood** (1831–1879): *An 1853 graduate of West Point, Hood gave General Lee his first victory when his Fourth Texas Brigade (Hood's Texas Brigade) routed Union forces at Gaines' Mill on May 28, 1862. Famous as a fighting general, in the fall of '62 he was transferred to Braxton Bragg's Army of Tennessee. He had his right leg shot away at Chickamauga. He commanded the Army of Tennessee against Sherman in the final months of the war, but requested that he be relieved of his command following his defeat at Nashville. After the war he became a cotton broker in New Orleans where he and his wife and daughter died in the yellow fever epidemic of 1879, leaving behind ten orphaned children.* (National Archives)

**Lieutenant General Leonidas Polk** (1806–1864): *An 1827 graduate of West Point, Polk was a classmate and dear friend of both Jefferson Davis and Albert Sidney Johnston who resigned his commission to become a bishop in the Episcopal Church. In '61 Davis named him commander of troops in western Tennessee and east Arkansas. His occupation of Columbus, Kentucky (instead of Paducah) has been called a "major catastrophe" of the war. Later he combined forces with Albert Sidney Johnston to form the Army of Tennessee, with Polk in command of the First Corps (which he led at Pittsburgh Landing). He disliked General Bragg intensely and became the leader of the anti–Bragg faction. He was killed at Pine Mountain, Georgia, in June of '64. (Indeed, Polk took time out from his fighting to baptize both John Bell Hood and Joe Johnston.)* (National Archives)

**The Battle Flag of General Leonidas Polk's Corps.** *It is noted that Polk created his own battle flag by reversing the colors and substituting the Roman Cross for the St. Andrew's Cross.* (Cannon, *Flags of the Confederacy*)

**Brigadier General John Hunt Morgan** (1825–1864): *A native of Lexington, Kentucky, young Morgan attended Transylvania University, and in 1860 organized the Lexington Rifles, a pro-southern local militia. In 1861 he joined the Confederacy, and a year later commanded a squadron of cavalry at Pittsburgh Landing. In December of '62 he was promoted to brigadier general and given command of the Second Kentucky Cavalry Regiment, which became famous throughout the North and South as Morgan's Raiders. It was said that the Raiders made Ohio and Indiana their personal battleground. He was captured at New Lisbon, Ohio, in July of '63, but in November he managed an incredible escape by tunneling out of the Ohio State Penitentiary. In December of '64, he led his men on a daring mission to Greenville, Tennessee, where he was killed.*

*At Christmas of 1862 General John Hunt Morgan, 36, wed the vivacious 17-year-old Mattie Ready at her home in Nashville. (Morgan's sister was married to General A. P. Hill.) It was considered a grand occasion, and among the wedding guests were President Jefferson Davis and Braxton Bragg. Even General Leonidas Polk put aside his uniform and donned the vestments of an Episcopal bishop long enough to conduct the ceremony.* (Photographs courtesy Library of Congress)

*John Hunt Morgan and his Raiders, famous for their fun-loving hijinks, enjoy a night on the town in this quaint Ohio village (according to this outrageous cartoon which appeared in an 1863 issue of* Harper's Weekly).

*In 1864, closely pursued by Union cavalry, Morgan attempted to hide in a vineyard in Greenville, Tennessee. Finally, when all was lost, he emerged with his hands raised in surrender. At that point he was cold-bloodedly shot to death by Private Andrew Campbell of the 13th Tennessee Union Cavalry. His body was then mutilated by jubilant Yankee soldiers. (Kentucky Cavaliers in Dixie)*

*These tall, rawboned southern lads of the 9th Mississippi Infantry Regiment fought with the Army of Tennessee throughout the war, and were with Johnston when the end came at Bentonville, N.C.* (Library of Congress)

*General Sterling Price's raiders, a unit of some 12,000 southerners, some gathered from as far away as Texas, during their invasion of Missouri late in the war. Artist Sam Reader was among the Federal prisoners depicted here, though he soon made his escape. It should be noted that the flag carried in this painting is a variation of Price's battle flag, one that Reader painted from memory some years after the fact. (In fact, this flag appears to be the battle flag of General Dabney H. Maury.)* (Kansas State Historical Society)

**Major General Sterling Price** (1809–1867): *Son of a wealthy family, Price was elected to Congress from Missouri in 1844, then served a term as governor. In 1860, despite his moderate stance on secession, he became annoyed at the radical position taken by Nathaniel Lyon, a Federal officer, and on June 11, 1861, joined by General Ben McCulloch and his Arkansas army, he mobilized state troops to oppose Federal soldiers marching on Springfield. On August 10, Price and McCulloch defeated Lyon and his Union forces at Oak Hills. Lyons was killed and Federal troops retreated from the area. In March of '62 Price and his troops joined the Army of the West under General Earl Van Dorn. Despite Van Dorn's defeat at Elkhorn Tavern, Price was promoted to major general for his outstanding performance in that battle. After participating in the fights at Iuka and Corinth, Price and his army joined General Kirby Smith in the successful Red River campaign. Late in the war he invaded Missouri, an incredible march of over 1,400 miles (this was the longest campaign of the war in terms of miles covered), but was finally forced back to Arkansas. At war's end, refusing to surrender his army, Price escaped to Mexico, where he founded Carlota, a colony of ex–Confederates. Two years later he returned to Missouri where he died in 1867.* (Library of Congress)

*Confederate flags bearing the Roman cross first gained popularity with the Missouri regiments of General Sterling Price's Army of the West and then spread to other units serving in that theater.* (Joseph Crute, *Emblems of Southern Valor*)

H. B. Granbury

John Adams

O. F. Strahl

Patrick Cleburne

States Rights Gist

**A Sad Day for the Confederacy:** *The above five Confederate generals were all killed on November 30, 1864, during Hood's terrible defeat at the Battle of Franklin. A sixth general, John C. Carter, was mortally wounded, and five others received lesser wounds, while a twelfth was captured.*

**Brigadier General Hiram Bronson Granbury** (1831–64): *A Mississippi native who moved to Waco, Texas, in 1857 to practice law. In 1861 he became a colonel with the Seventh Texas Infantry. In the fall of '63 Granbury was sent to Atlanta with Johnston's Army of Tennessee. Then came General Hood and the Seventh's ill-fated fight at Franklin. (He was buried in Granbury, Texas, a town named in his honor.)*

**Brigadier General Otho French Strahl** (1831–64): *A native of Ohio and a graduate of Ohio Wesleyan University, Strahl was practicing law in Nashville when the war broke out. He was given the rank of colonel and assigned to the Fourth Tennessee Infantry Regiment attached to the Army of Tennessee. In July of '63 he was promoted to brigadier general, given command of a brigade and badly wounded at Atlanta. He returned to duty just in time to participate in the Battle of Franklin.*

**Brigadier General John Adams** (1825–64): *A career military officer graduating from West Point in 1845, in '61 Adams was placed in command of southern troops in Memphis. In May of '62 he was given command of six Mississippi infantry regiments and assigned to the Army of Tennessee. He, too, joined Hood's army following the Atlanta campaign.*

**Major General Patrick Ronayne Cleburne** (1828–64): *A native of Ireland, Cleburne spent a year in the British army before buying his discharge and sailing for New Orleans. In 1855 he began practicing law in Helena, Arkansas, then in 1861 became a captain in the First Arkansas Infantry. That fall the First Arkansas joined Hardee's army and marched to Bowling Green where it became a part of Albert Sidney Johnston's army. There, Cleburne was given command of a brigade in Hardee's Third Corps, which he turned into one of the finest brigades in the entire army. At Shiloh Cleburne lost over 50 percent of his command. At Perryville he was twice wounded but promoted to major general and given command of a division. After Atlanta he was placed in command of Hardee's entire corps, and performed brilliantly at Chickamauga. Then it was on to Franklin where Cleburne had two horses shot out from under him before a Union bullet ended his life.* (Library of Congress)

**Brigadier General States Rights Gist** (1810–64): *A native of Union, S.C., Gist's father, the governor of South Carolina, was a disciple of John C. Calhoun and chose his son's name to reflect his political leanings. In 1861 Gist was appointed adjutant general of the South Carolina Militia. In July of '61 he served as aide-de-camp to General Bernard Bee at the First Manassas, but when all the officers of the Fourth Alabama went down either dead or wounded, Gist took command of that regiment for the rest of the battle. Assigned to the Army of Tennessee, he commanded a brigade at Chickamauga in September of '63. He too was killed at the Battle of Franklin and is buried at the Trinity Episcopal Church Cemetery in Columbia.* (Library of Congress)

**Major General Benjamin F. Cheatham** (1820–86): *A native of Nashville, Cheatham fought in the Mexican War and later panned for gold in California. As commander of the Provisional Army of Tennessee, Cheatham and his force distinguished themselves in most of the great western battles: Pittsburg Landing, Chaplin Hills, Chickamauga, Murfreesboro, and the Atlanta campaigns. He and Braxton Bragg soon became sworn enemies, and Bragg broke up Cheatham's division after Chickamauga. But Joe Johnston restored the division when he replaced Bragg. Later Cheatham was given command of Hardee's corps during Hood's invasion of Tennessee. Following the war he became superintendent of the Tennessee prison system.* (Library of Congress)

**Brigadier General Thomas Logan** (1840–1914): *He graduated from the South Carolina College in 1860 (he served as class salutatorian), then volunteered as a private in the Hampton Legion. He was promoted to general at the age of 24, the youngest general officer in the Confederate Army. He was at Bentonville with Johnston at war's end and it is said that his unit made the last cavalry charge of the war. He moved to Richmond in 1866, founded the Southern Railway, and became a very wealthy man and a close associate of John D. Rockefeller.* (South Caroliniana Library, University of South Carolina)

**Brigadier General John Pegram** (West Point, 1854): *A colonel with the 20th Virginia Infantry, Pegram was captured and paroled at Rich Mountain in 1861. He was then assigned to General Bragg's staff in Tupelo as chief of engineers. A short time later he became chief of staff to General Kirby Smith. Noted for his intelligence and daring, he was next assigned to Nathan Bedford Forrest and led a cavalry brigade at both Chickamauga and Murfreesboro. Then it was back to northern Virginia where he commanded an infantry brigade under Jubal Early. He was killed at Hatcher's Run on February 6, 1865, only a few days following his wedding to Hetty Cary, and only weeks before war's end.* (National Archives)

**Major General Matthew C. Butler** (1836–1909): *He was one of several students expelled from the South Carolina College in 1856 for his role in the Guard House Riot. He married Governor Francis Pickens' daughter in 1858 and became an officer in the Hampton Legion in 1861. Despite losing his leg at Brandy Station in '63, he took command of the Hampton Legion in '64, and was considered one of the South's most outstanding cavalry leaders. He was with Johnston's army when the end came in April '65. Following the war he would serve in the U.S. Senate and was appointed a general in the U.S. Army in 1898.* (South Caroliniana Library, University of South Carolina)

**Brigadier General James Cantey** (1818–1874): *A South Carolinian who served as an officer in the Palmetto Regiment during the Mexican War, in 1861 he became commander of the Fifteenth Alabama Infantry. He served under Stonewall Jackson in the Shenandoah, and participated in the fighting around Richmond during '62 where he was credited with the southern victory at Cross Keys. In December of '62 he moved to Mobile where he organized a brigade to defend that city. In the winter of '64 his brigade joined the Army of Tennessee and helped defend Atlanta. Then he joined General Johnston against Sherman in the Carolinas. Following the war, refusing to request a pardon, he returned to his farm in Alabama.* (Library of Congress)

**Major General Joe "Fighting Joe" Wheeler** (1836–1906): *An 1859 graduate of West Point, in 1862 Wheeler was placed in command of cavalry in Bragg's army of Mississippi and Tennessee. Following the death of Jeb Stuart in May of '64 Wheeler became the ranking cavalry leader in the Confederacy. In early 1865 it was Wheeler's cavalry that offered the only organized resistance to Sherman's march through Georgia. He and his cavalry troops then returned to Richmond and escorted Jefferson Davis and his Cabinet on their flight from the Capital. (He later remarked that one of his fondest memories was of carrying the Davises' infant daughter in his arms during their attempted escape.) After the war he served eight terms in the U.S. House of Representatives from Alabama, then served as a general in the U.S. Army during the war with Spain.* (National Archives)

# 3

# Troops

*These brave lads of the Confederacy were photographed in 1861, early in the conflict, when they were well clothed, well fed, and well equipped. By the spring of '64, such units were composed of barefoot boys and bearded old men. They were ragged, starved, and diseased, armed with little more than spirit and a grim determination to protect their families and homes from the Northern invader. They are still remembered as the greatest infantry the world has ever seen. (Library of Congress)*

*These typical young Southerners, finding humor in the grimmest of situations, have nailed a sign reading "Beauregard's Mess" to the door of the dilapidated shack in the background.* (The Austin History Center)

**"Leaving Home,"** *a painting by famous Southern artist Gilbert Gaul. Because of its rich use of symbolism, this work better captures the spirit of the Old South than any other painting from the Civil War era.* (Birmingham Museum of Art)

### A Georgia Volunteer
Mary Ashley Townsend (1832–1901)

*Far up the lonely mountain-side*
*My wandering footsteps led;*
*The moss lay thick beneath my feet,*
*The pine sighed overhead.*
*The trace of a dismantled fort*
*Lay in the forest nave,*
*And in the shadow near my path*
*I saw a soldier's grave.*
*The bramble wrestled with the weed*
*Upon the lowly mound;*
*The simple head-board, rudely writ,*
*Had rotted to the ground;*
*I raised it with a reverent hand,*
*From dust its words to clear,*
*But time had blotted all but these —*
*"A Georgia Volunteer!"*
*I saw the toad and scaly snake*
*From tangled covert start,*
*And hide themselves among the weed*
*Above the dead man's heart;*
*But undisturbed, in sleep profound,*
*Unheeding, there he lay;*
*His coffin but the mountain soil,*
*His shroud Confederate gray.*
*I heard the Shenandoah roll*
*Along the vale below,*
*I saw the Alleghanies rise*
*Towards the realms of snow.*
*The "Valley Campaign" rose to mind —*
*Its leader's name — and then*
*I knew the sleeper had been one*
*Of Stonewall Jackson's men.*
*Yet whence he came, what lip shall say —*
*Whose tongue will ever tell*
*What desolated hearths and hearts*

*Have been because he fell?*
*What sad-eyed maiden braids her hair,*
*Her hair which he held dear?*
*One lock of which perchance lies with*
*The Georgia Volunteer?*
*What mother, with long watching eyes,*
*And white lips cold and dumb,*
*Waits with appalling patience for*
*Her darling boy to come?*
*Her boy! whose mountain grave swells up*
*But one of many a scar,*
*Cut on the face of our fair land,*
*By gory-handed war.*
*What fights he fought, what wounds he wore,*
*Are all unknown to fame;*
*Remember, on his lonely grave*
*There is not e'en a name!*
*That he fought well and bravely too,*
*And held his country dear,*
*We know, else he had never been*
*A Georgia Volunteer.*
*He sleeps — what need to question now*
*If he were wrong or right?*
*He knows, ere this, whose cause was just*
*In God the Father's sight.*
*He wields no warlike weapons now,*
*Returns no foeman's thrust —*
*Who but a coward would revile*
*An honest soldier's dust?*
*Roll, Shenandoah, proudly roll,*
*Adown the rocky glen,*
*Above thee lies the grave of one*
*of Stonewall Jackson's men.*
*Beneath the cedar and the pine,*
*In solitude austere,*
*Unknown, unnamed, forgotten lies*
*A Georgia Volunteer.*

## *The Texas Rangers*

**The Texas Rangers (8th Texas Cavalry), generally referred to as Terry's Texas Rangers.** This heroic band of Rangers was organized by Ben Terry and Thomas Lubbock with some 1,170 men in Houston, Texas, on September 9, 1861. It was said that the Rangers enlisted for "the duration of the war" and were "the best that Texas had to offer." For the most part the men of the Rangers were in their teens and early twenties, and each man furnished his own arms and horse. As in most Confederate regiments the men elected their own officers, though they paid little attention to rank. They served initially with Gen. Albert Sidney Johnston in the Western Theater, and later with generals Joe Wheeler, John Wharton, and Thomas Harrison in the Army of Tennessee, and took heavy casualties at Pittsburgh Landing, Murfreesboro, Chickamauga, and later at Knoxville and Atlanta. At war's end they fought in the defense of Savannah and the Carolinas. Of their original number, only about 30 survivors surrendered with General Johnston in North Carolina in 1865.

**Brigadier General Benjamin Franklin Terry,** *organizer of Terry's Texas Rangers (8th Texas Cavalry). They were described by one general as "the equal of the Old Guard of Napoleon" and by another as "a damned armed mob." The gallant Terry was killed in Kentucky in December of 1861 in his Rangers' first charge of the war.* (Texas Ranger Museum, Waco)

(Joseph Crute, *Emblems of Southern Valor*)

**Terry's Texas Rangers** *would carry the Bonnie Blue Flag early in the war, but later would switch to a flag bearing the Roman cross so popular with Sterling Price's troops of the Trans-Mississippi theater.* (Texas Ranger Museum, Waco)

**Major General John A. Wharton** (1825–1865), *a native Texan and a graduate of the South Carolina College. Following the death of General Terry, Wharton led the Rangers at Pittsburgh Landing under General Albert Sidney Johnston. Later he and his Rangers served with generals Joe Wheeler and Nathan Bedford Forrest at Murfreesboro and Chickamauga. Indeed, despite his lack of military training, Wharton became one of the South's top generals. In April of '65, he died at General Magruder's headquarters in Houston, shot dead by Colonel George Baylor during a violent argument. Baylor testified that Wharton called him a liar, then slapped his face.* (South Caroliniana Library, University of South Carolina)

**The Rev. Robert Franklin Bunting,** *a Presbyterian minister, was a native of Pennsylvania and from a family of staunch abolitionists. Yet he so strongly believed in States' Rights that he threw in his lot with the South. Here he wears the silver star of Terry's Texas Rangers.* (The Texas Ranger Museum, Waco)

**Battle Flag of Parson's Texas Cavalry** (Joseph Crute, *Emblems of Southern Valor*)

**Song of the Texas Rangers**
By J. D. Young

(Sung to the tune of
"The Yellow Rose of Texas")

*The morning star is paling, the campfires flicker low;*
*Our steeds are madly neighing; for the bugle bids us go:*
*So put the foot in stirrup and shake the bridle free,*
*For today the Texas Rangers must cross the Tennessee.*
*With Wharton for our leader, we'll chase the dastard foe,*
*Till our horses bathe their fetlocks in the deep, blue Ohio.*

*'Tis joy to be a Ranger! to fight for dear Southland!*
*'Tis joy to follow Wharton, with his gallant, trusty band!*
*'Tis joy to see our Harrison plunge, like a meteor bright,*
*Into the thickest of the fray, and deal his deadly might.*
*O! who'd not be a Ranger and follow Wharton's cry*
*And battle for his country, and, if needs be, die?*

*Above:* **These Texas Rangers** *and thousands of others like them distinguished themselves on all fronts throughout the war. Remnants of these gallant regiments surrendered with Joe Johnston's army at Bentonville in April of '65.* (Texas Ranger Museum, Waco)

**The Second Texas Infantry,** *their battle flag proudly waving alongside the Stars and Bars, attacks Battery Robinette at the Battle of Corinth in desperate hand-to-hand combat. (A detail from a lithograph by Kurz and Allison of Chicago, 1870.)* (Civil War Times Illustrated)

### The Burial of Latane

*...in accents soft and low,*
*Trembling with pity, touched with pathos, read*
*Over his hallowed dust the ritual for the dead.*

*Let us not weep for him, whose deeds endure;*
*So young; so brave, so beautiful; he died*
*As he had wished to die — the past is sure.*
*Whatever yet of sorrow may betide*
*Those who still linger by the stormy shore,*
*Change cannot touch him now, or fortune harm him more.*

*And when Virginia, leaning on her spear —*
*"Victrix et Vidua," the conflict done —*
*Shall raise her mailed hand to wipe the tear*
*That starts as she recalls each martyred son,*
*No prouder memory her breast shall sway*
*Than thine, our early lost, lamented LATANE.*

*Reputed to be perhaps the most popular print from the war, "The Burial of Latane" tells the story of a young cavalry officer, Dr. William Latane, a Virginian and a member of Stuart's Cavalry, who was killed at Linney's Corner during the Peninsular Campaign of 1862. His body was taken to a nearby plantation owned by a Dr. Brockenborough and left there with women, children and slaves, the only civilians available at that point in the war, and given a Christian burial. In 1929* The Confederate Veteran *stated that no other print from the war better captured the "spirit of the women of the South" than did this print. (Southern beauty Constance Cary, who made one of the original battle flags, served as a model for the young lady fifth from right in this work.)* (Collection of Judge John E. DeHardit, The Museum of the Confederacy, Richmond. Photograph by Katherine Wetzel)

**The Stars and Bars** *waves proudly over Confederate forces at Sharpsburg, Maryland, on September 17, 1862. The South finally wrested victory from the North, thanks to the arrival of General A. P. Hill's Light Division after an incredible seven-hour, seventeen-mile march. They then hit Burnside's left flank and the stunned Federals fled in defeat. Indeed, September 17, 1862, is still remembered as the single bloodiest day of the war as some 23,000 Union and Confederate troops went down in less than 12 hours.* (Thomas Cooper Library, University of South Carolina)

*With the Texas Rangers on the one hand and the Cherokee Mounted Rifles on the other, the Yankees had their hands full at Elkhorn Tavern.* (The Confederate Museum, Richmond. Photograph by Katherine Wetzel)

*Hunt Wilson, a Confederate artilleryman, painted this scene of his battery under attack at Elkhorn Tavern on the second day of fighting.* (The Confederate Museum, Richmond. Photograph by Katherine Wetzel)

*It is little remembered today but prior to the war Earl Van Dorn was considered an accomplished musician and artist. His niece Mary Ann Lacy sat for the above oil portrait ("Lady with a Dagger") in 1858.* (Civil War Times Illustrated)

## Native Americans of the Confederacy

**Brigadier General Stand Watie** (1806–1871): *Chief of the Western Cherokees, he led his regiment in several engagements in the Indian Territory before being sent to Arkansas where they joined General Van Dorn at Elkhorn Tavern in March of '62. In all, the Cherokee Mounted Rifles participated in eighteen engagements during the war. Watie finally surrendered his regiment on June 23, 1865, the last Confederate general to lay down his arms. He then lived the quiet life of a farmer until his death in 1871. Watie was the only Native American general officer on either side during the entire war.* (Medford, Oklahoma, Historical Society)

**Oklahoma Cherokees** *wounded at Elkhorn Tavern receive medical attention behind the lines. It was said that they were excellent combat soldiers but, much like their white Southern counterparts, did not take well to discipline and regimentation.* (Library of Congress)

**CSA Indian Commissioner General Albert Pike,** *briefly commanded Cherokee regiments in Arkansas. He resigned his position with the Confederacy in 1862.* (National Archives)

**John Ross,** *a well-known Cherokee chief who fought for the Confederacy.* (Oklahoma Historical Society)

**Colonel Adair and Captain Scraper:** *Cherokees who fought under General Stand Watie for the Confederacy.* (Smithsonian Institution)

**Colonel James Downing and Major John Drew:** *Both veterans of the Battle of Elkhorn Tavern. Downing was a tribal chief with the Cherokees and Drew a Cherokee merchant.* (Oklahoma Historical Society)

**The Thomas Legion:** *Composed of two companies of Cherokees from the Blue Ridge Mountains of North Carolina, the Legion fought bravely throughout the war in eastern Tennessee and western North Carolina under the command of Colonel William H. Thomas, a white citizen soldier. Here survivors of the Thomas Legion enjoy a reunion in 1907.* (Museum of the Cherokee Nation, Cherokee, N.C.)

"**That Devil**" *Forrest's cavalry makes a daring charge at Pittsburg Landing. A much-frustrated General Sherman once said, "If Forrest would take his men to Alaska, I'd agree to feed and supply them every day for the next ten years."* (The Museum of the Confederacy, New Orleans)

***Opposite:*** **The C.S.S.** ***Hunley,*** *the world's first submarine, sank the U.S.S.* Housatonic *off the coast of Charleston in February 1864. The* Hunley, *along with her crew, was sunk in the process. The* Hunley *was raised in the summer of 2000 and is now on display in Charleston, S.C. In this Conrad Wise Chapman painting the sub's inventor, Jacob Hunley, is standing with his arm resting on the sub's rudder.* (The Museum of the Confederacy, Richmond. Photograph by Katherine Wetzel)

*A world away from homes and families, these despondent Confederate veterans captured at Chattanooga await railway transportation to a Federal prison in Rock Island, Illinois. Despite constant pleas from the Confederacy, after 1863 the Federal government refused to exchange prisoners, leaving their own men to suffer in southern prisoner of war camps.* (National Archives)

***Opposite*: The High Tide of the Confederacy.** *The brigades of generals James Kemper, Richard Garnett, and Lewis Armistead spearheaded Pickett's charge at Gettysburg. Kemper and Garnett quickly went down mortally wounded, but Armistead's men finally mounted the stone wall on Cemetery Ridge. At that point Armistead yelled, "Give them the cold steel, boys! Who will follow me?" Moments later he, too, was mortally wounded by a Yankee bullet. In this painting General Armistead can be seen in the middle foreground, hat on sword.* (Gettysburg National Military Park)

**Pvt. Andrew Hoge:** *A sharpshooter with the 4th Virginia Infantry, he was killed by shrapnel at Gettysburg on July 3, 1863. He had time to spread his blanket beneath him before he bled to death. He had just turned eighteen.* (National Archives)

**Three of the 2,500 Southerners captured at Gettysburg.** *A Philadelphia journalist wrote of them: "They were the dirtiest men I ever saw, a most ragged, lean and hungry set of wolves. Yet there was a certain dash about them that the northern men seemed to lack."* (National Archives)

**Major John "The Gallant" Pelham:** *He resigned from West Point two weeks prior to graduation in 1861 to accept a commission in the Confederate Army (he's wearing his West Point uniform in this photograph.) He was in command of Jeb Stuart's artillery when he was killed at Kelly's Ford in '63, two weeks shy of his 21st birthday.* (Cook Collection, Valentine Museum)

**Private E. F. Jennison:** *A Georgia volunteer, he was killed at Malvern Hill. He had just turned sixteen.* (Library of Congress)

**Men of Company A,** *5th Georgia Volunteers lounge about in camp in this photograph taken in Augusta, Georgia, in 1861. The letters "CR" on the tent stand for Clinch Rifles, the company's name. In November of 1863, the 5th Georgia lost over 60 percent of its men at Chickamauga. What remained of this brave unit then fought on doggedly with Hood and Johnston until war's end, finally surrendering at Bentonville, N.C., on April 26, 1865.* (Georgia Historical Society, Savannah)

***Opposite:*** *On July 4, 1863, following a 47-day siege, General John Pemberton surrendered Vicksburg to General Grant. The suffering in that city had been terrible, and in addition to the thousands who died in combat, many women and children died of starvation.* (Old Courthouse Museum, Vicksburg)

**Lads of the celebrated Fifth Company, Washington Artillery of New Orleans:** *The Washington Artillery furnished four companies to the Army of Northern Virginia, but the Fifth Company was assigned to General Braxton Bragg's Army of the Mississippi and surrendered with the fall of Vicksburg.* (The Photographic History of the Civil War)

**Flag of the Fifth Company, Washington Artillery of New Orleans.** (Confederate Memorial Hall, New Orleans)

**Tattered by months of Federal bombardments,** *the Stainless Banner flies defiantly over Fort Sumter in 1863, in the Conrad Wise Chapman painting entitled "The Flag of Fort Sumter, October 20, 1863."* (The Confederate Museum, Richmond. Photograph by Katherine Wetzel)

**Private John Thomas Stone,** *a native of Manning, S.C., was a lad of twenty when this photograph was taken in 1861. He served with the Santee Guerrillas in 1860–61, but with the outbreak of war he became a member of Company H, Fifth South Carolina Cavalry. His younger brother, Lawrence Stone, was killed at the Battle of Salkahatchie in 1862. Stone himself would later tell harrowing tales of his service as a mounted courier on Morris Island in July of 1863. He survived the war and went on to father twenty children prior to his death in 1921. (He is the author's great-grandfather.)* (John Chandler Griffin)

*In this remarkable shot by Charleston photographer G. S. Cook, South Carolina troops may be seen sitting among the rubble of Fort Sumter in October 1863 following months of bombardment from the Union blockading fleet anchored in Charleston Harbor. (Library of Congress)*

**Opposite:** *In this Louis Kurz painting these gallant Confederate forces storm a Federal fortification at Fort Sanders near Knoxville in November of 1863. (Andrew Mollo Collection)*

## Quantrill's Raiders

**Captain William Quantrill,** *a school teacher from Dover, Ohio, and a notorious guerrilla leader who terrorized Union forces (and Union sympathizers) in Kansas, Missouri, and Kentucky throughout the war. Among the more infamous of his troops were the James and Younger brothers. He was murdered by Federal soldiers when he attempted to surrender his band in May of 1865. (Oddly enough, his skull is now on display in the Dover County Museum.)* (Library of Congress)

**The Youngers in 1874:** *From the left: James, sister Rhetta, Robert and Cole. Their brother John had just been killed.*

*In 1861 a band of Kansas Jayhawkers robbed their wealthy father of $4,000 worth of carriages and horses. A month later Cole and his brothers joined Quantrill's Raiders. (In 1862 a Union captain shot and killed their father in retaliation.) Cole was present when the Raiders killed 150 boys and men in Lawrence, Kansas, in August 1863. A month later he joined the regular Confederate Army and spent the rest of the war as an army recruiter in New Mexico.*

*Following the war the Youngers joined with Frank and Jesse James to rob federal banks. John was killed in 1874, and in 1876 the others were captured in Northfield, Minnesota, and sentenced to life in prison. Bob died in jail, but Jim and Cole were released in 1901. Jim committed suicide that same year, but Cole lived until 1916.* (Library of Congress)

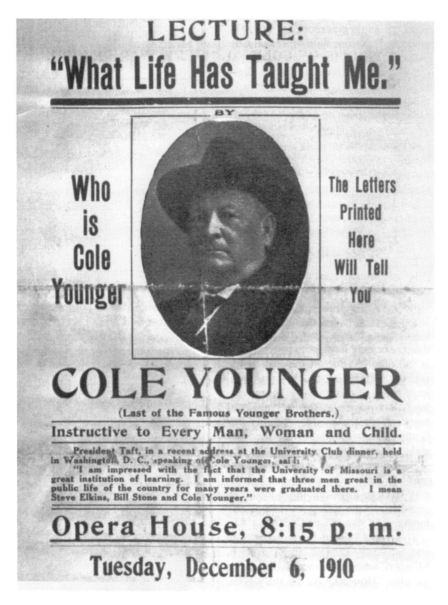

**Cole Younger:** *He served 25 years in a Minnesota prison following a foiled 1876 bank robbery. Upon his parole in 1901 a reformed Cole Younger joined with Frank James in a wild west show and made a good living delivering spiritual lectures to audiences across America.* (Jackson County Historical Society)

Frank "Buck" James and Jesse "Dingus" James: *Notorious members of Quantrill's Raiders and the most famous bank robbers in history. Jesse was only seventeen when this photo was taken, Frank twenty-one. They were raised in a Christian home and it is said that neither drank, smoked nor used profanity. Indeed their father was the Rev. Robert James, a founder of William Jewell College, a highly respected liberal arts institution. Jesse would be assassinated in St. Joseph, Missouri, in 1882, shot by Bob Ford, a trusted traitor.* (Missouri State Historical Society)

*Following Jesse's assassination in 1882, hometown juries would twice try and acquit Frank James of numerous crimes. By 1914, now a respectable senior citizen, he would charge tourists fifty cents to tour the James' boyhood farm ("KODAKS BARED") in Clay County, Missouri. (He also played minor roles in several Hollywood films.)* (Missouri State Historical Society)

**Gaylord Blair Clark (*left*) and Thomas G. Jefferson (*right*):** *Two of the valiant young VMI cadets mustered into service to fight Federal forces at New Market in the Shenandoah Valley. Both young men were only seventeen at the time of the battle. (Jefferson was the great-grandson of President Thomas Jefferson.)* (The VMI Archives, Lexington)

**Colonel Scott Shipp** *commanded the brave lads of VMI during their daylong fight at New Market. He himself was only twenty-four at the time.* (New Market Battlefield Memorial)

"Charge of the VMI Cadets at New Market" *now hangs in Jackson Memorial Hall at Virginia Military Institute. The Confederacy had controlled the Shenandoah Valley since Stonewall Jackson's great campaigns of 1861–63, but in May of '64 the Union made another push to secure the Valley for themselves, prompting the VMI cadets to volunteer their services. At the Battle of New Market these lads, many of them only fifteen and sixteen years old, performed gallantly. When the moment came to order them into line, General Breckingridge turned to an aide and said softly, "Major, order them up and God forgive me for the order." Among their many other heroic exploits that day they overran and captured a battery of Federal artillery. It has been said that their actions saved not only the Shenandoah but perhaps Lee's army as well. Of the 600 cadets involved in this engagement, 57 were killed or wounded.* (Benjamin West Clinedinst, New Market Battlefield Park)

**Colonel John Singleton Mosby (The Gray Ghost):** *A Bristol, La., attorney prior to the war, he initially served as a scout for Stuart's cavalry. Later, he and his Partisan Rangers (43rd Battalion of Virginia Cavalry) became notorious throughout the North for their lightning thrusts behind Union lines, and quickly earned the reputation as the most successful southern guerrilla unit of the entire war. Following General Lee's surrender, Moseby received a parole from General Grant himself. He then became a senior agent for the United States Department of Justice.* (Valentine Museum, Richmond)

A few more of Mosby's Raiders: *( L–R) John Munson, Ben Palmer, Thomas Booker, Walter Gosden and A. G. Babcock. (Walter Gosden would later become the father of Freeman Gosden, known to millions of twentieth century radio listeners as "Amos" on the nationally famous "Amos 'n Andy Show.")* (Cook Collection, Valentine Museum)

*Opposite*: The daredevil Colonel John Mosby (center) and his Partisan Rangers: *A unit composed primarily of Marylanders. They are best remembered perhaps for capturing Union General Edwin H. Stoughton asleep in his bed at Fairfax Court House in March of 1863. (Note: an occupying Yankee army prevented Maryland from exercising her right to secede from the Union, but the vast majority of her young men became members of the Confederate Army.)* (Maryland Historical Society)

*This brave southern boy, still surrounded by all the accouterments of war, was hit twice by enemy bullets at Spotsylvania. He used his shirt to stanch the flow of blood from the wound in his leg, but he eventually bled to death from the wound in his shoulder, which suggests, sadly enough, that he died alone.* (National Archives)

*Opposite*: **Moseby and his Rangers (the 43rd Virginia Cavalry)** *return triumphantly from a raid on a Union supply train in the Valley in the autumn of 1864. The Yankee prisoners in the foreground do not appear quite as jubilant as their captors.* (National Archives)

*On March 22, 1864, near Dalton, Georgia, Major General Benjamin Cheatham's Tennessee Division, typical southerners, took time out from their deadly struggles with Sherman's army to square off for a snowball fight with Major General W. H. T. Walker's 41st Georgia Division. The 41st Georgia briefly lost its flag (below) to the Volunteers.* (The Confederate Veteran)

**The battle flag of the 41st Georgia Infantry.** *By war's end this was all that remained of their glorious banner.* (The Museum of the Confederacy, Richmond. Photograph by Katherine Wetzel)

**Brigadier General Micah Jenkins** (1835–64): *Called one of the South's best and brightest, he was an 1854 graduate of The Citadel (first in his class), who then started his own military academy in Yorkville, S.C. At the First Manassas he led the Sixth South Carolina Infantry and was credited with forcing McDowell's retreat. A year later he was given command of Hood's Division after Hood was severely wounded at Chickamauga. He distinguished himself for gallantry in that great battle and was promoted to brigadier general. He later commanded a brigade in Lee's Army of Northern Virginia and was killed during the Battle of the Wilderness on May 6, 1864.* (South Caroliniana Library, University of South Carolina)

**Micah Jenkins took command** *of General Hood's Texas Division following Hood's terrible wounding at Chickamauga. Here, Confederate cavalry and infantry run into a veritable hornet's nest of Union activity during that battle, a great victory for the South.* (Confederate Museum)

## The Confederate Secret Service

Jacob Thompson, director of the Confederate Secret Service in Canada: *He began his operations in Montreal in May of 1864. Among its many other daring exploits, the Secret Service attempted to free Confederate prisoners of war from northern prisons, to fuel discontent among Northern Copperheads, and to raid American cities along the Canadian border in hopes of provoking the Federal government into invading Canada. Unfortunately, the Secret Service was plagued from the very beginning by internal strife, betrayals, and Federal agents sent to Montreal to monitor their movements. It is said that Confederate agents became so well known to their Federal counterparts that they were sometimes observed gaily socializing with one another in various Montreal hotels and barrooms. Following the assassination of Abraham Lincoln, Thompson, armed with over $300,000 in Confederate gold, fled to England where he remained for the next four years. To date, the Confederate gold has never been accounted for.* (Library of Congress)

**Lieutenant Bennett H. Young** (*far right*): *A Kentucky cavalry officer and leader of the Confederate raid on St. Albans, he poses with other members of his band as they await trial for murder and bank robbery in a Montreal jail. A Canadian judge ruled, however, that the raiders were engaged in an act of war and that the money they took from various St. Albans banks should be returned to the raiders. (It is said that the packed courtroom erupted in "rebel yells" when the judge's decision was announced.)* (St. Albans Historical Society)

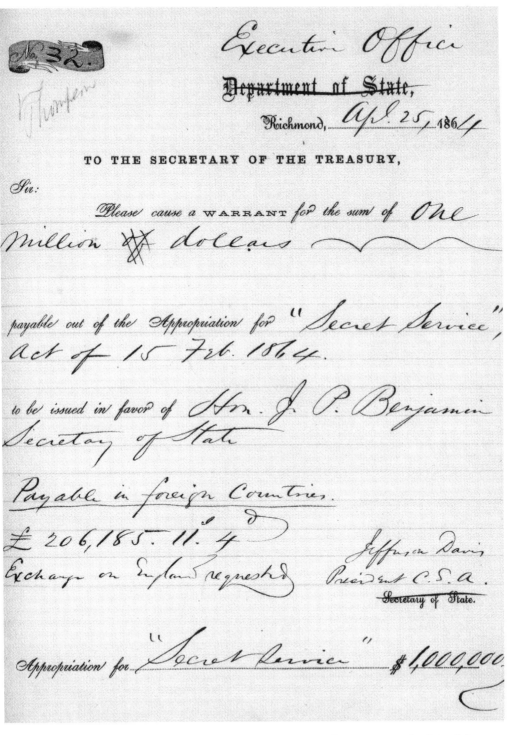

*Dated April 25, 1864, this bank draft was signed by President Jefferson Davis to fund Confederate Secret Service operations in Canada.* (Library of Congress)

**Clement Clay:** *A former U.S. senator from Alabama and second in command to Jacob Thompson in Canada. Compounding problems for the Confederate Secret Service, Clay and Thompson were old enemies who refused to speak to one another and generally worked at cross purposes. Indeed, the CSA could not have chosen a more unlikely couple than these two to head up its covert operations north of the border.* (National Archives)

**William Moultrie Dwight,** *a former cadet at The Citadel, was wounded at First Manassas, was twice captured, and later served as inspector general under General Joseph Kershaw. After the war he was elected mayor of Winnsboro, S.C., and then became a college president.* (The Citadel Archives)

Captain M. B. Humphrey, *commander of the Cadet Rangers.* (The Citadel Archives)

**Cadets from the South Carolina Military Acadamy (The Citadel)** *turned back the* Star of the West *when it attempted to supply Fort Sumter early in 1861. Then, in June of 1862, led by Captain M. B. Humphrey, 44 cadets left The Citadel under the cover of darkness and, against strict orders formed Company F, 6th South Carolina Cavalry (the Cadet Rangers). Assigned to the Hampton Legion, the cadets fought valiantly in most of the major campaigns of northern Virginia, then returned to South Carolina with Wade Hampton in 1865 in an effort to turn back Sherman's army. Following General Lee's surrender, Captain Humphrey and his cadets laid plans to join Kirby Smith and continue the war from Texas. But General Johnston's surrender eight days later destroyed that plan.*

*(Oddly enough, The Citadel still treats the Cadet Rangers as deserters from that august institution.)*

**Mary Boykin Chesnut** (1823–86): *A native of Camden, S.C., she was ardently opposed to slavery and authored the Civil War classic* A Diary from Dixie, *a veritable Who's-Who of the Confederacy. Her husband, Colonel John Chesnut, negotiated the surrender of Fort Sumter, and later became a member of Davis' Cabinet.* (Frontispiece, A Diary from Dixie)

**Captain Sally L. Tompkins** (1833–1916): *Founded a CSA hospital in Richmond in 1861. Since military hospitals had to be governed by military personnel, President Davis officially commissioned her a captain of cavalry, and thus Tompkins became the only woman to hold a commission in the Confederate Army. Following the war she dedicated her life to religious and charitable works, and was active in the Daughters of the Confederacy. Upon her death she was buried with full military honors in Richmond.* (National Archives)

**Mrs. Rose Greenhow** (1815–64): *Owner of a Washington boarding house, she gave information to General Beauregard that helped the South win at First Manassas, and was arrested by the Union Secret Service. (She is pictured here with her daughter at Old Capitol Prison.) Upon her release she sailed for England as an emissary for the South. Upon her return to America in 1864 she drowned when the blockade runner on which she was a passenger went down off the coast of Wilmington, N.C.* (The Naval Historical Center, Washington, D.C.)

**Belle Boyd** (1844–1900): *A daring Confederate spy whose exploits kept Stonewall Jackson well informed of Federal movements in the Shenandoah. In 1864 she sailed for England carrying Confederate dispatches when her ship was captured by a Union vessel commanded by Colonel Sam Hardin. She later married Hardin, who died in 1866, and worked as an actress until her death in 1900.* (Brady-Handy Collection, Library of Congress)

*This southern soldier, a beardless lad of fourteen, wearing neither shoes nor uniform, died of a bayonet wound at Fort Mahone in March of '65. A mere boy, he typifies the average Confederate soldier of 1865. One can only wonder what he might have become, should he have survived that terrible war.* (Library of Congress)

**Thousands of unknown soldiers:** *The war rolled on and southern boys continued to die by the thousands. This lad fell in a muddy trench at Petersburg. Who he was, where he was from, no one knows.* (Library of Congress)

# 4

# Major Battles

As a result of the attack on Fort Sumter, Lincoln immediately issued a call for 75,000 militia troops from the various states. The responses from the governors of those states that had remained loyal to the Union were positive. But the governor of Kentucky replied with a sneer that the Bluegrass State would furnish no troops "for the wicked purpose of subduing her sister Southern States." The governor of North Carolina wired, "You can get no troops from North Carolina." And Claiborne Fox Jackson, the governor of Missouri, wired that Lincoln's requisition was "illegal, unconstitutional, and revolutionary in its object, inhuman and diabolical, and cannot be complied with." Tennessee refused to furnish a single soldier "for purpose of coercion, but 50,000 for the defense of our rights and those of our southern brethren."

When the Confederate secretary of war, Leroy P. Walker of Alabama, put out a similar call for southern troops, the governors of the seceded states promised to send all the volunteers they could equip.

## 1861— Northern Virginia

**Big Bethel (Virginia), June 10, 1861:** The war was less than two months old when this first significant military action occurred. But Federal forces continued to hold Ft. Monroe, commanded by Gen. Ben Butler, at the tip of the Virginia Peninsula. Eight miles to the northwest Confederates had constructed a battery emplacement on the Black River at Big Bethel Church, manned by 1,400 men of the First North Carolina Regiment under Col. D. H. Hill. Thus, on June 10, Butler dispatched 4,400 soldiers under Gen. Pierce to drive them out.

Everything went wrong for the Federals from the beginning. In the early morning darkness men forgot the watchword; their white identification badges could not be seen in the darkness; some units became lost; then two regiments collided in the night

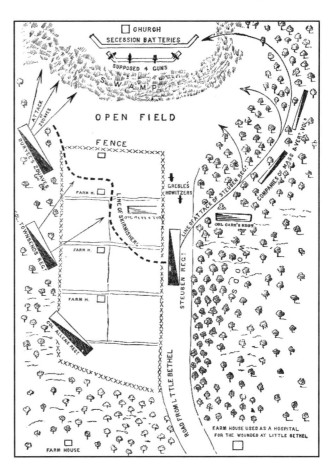

Big Bethel (Virginia), June 10, 1861.

and began firing at each other, alerting Confederates of their presence. By ten that morning, with the temperature hovering at ninety degrees, the Federals began a half-hearted assault on the Confederate battery. The southerners were hiding in the under-brush and immediately began raking the Federals with musket and cannon fire. Col. Hill later reported that his southern troops "were in high glee, and seemed to enjoy it as much as boys do rabbit-shooting."

Thirty minutes later the battle was over, with Pierce's men fleeing back to their camp, totally routed. Union casualties were 18 killed, 53 wounded and five missing. The Confederates had one killed and seven wounded. (See battle map.)

**First Manassas, July 21, 1861:** By the early summer of '61 the Confederacy had moved its seat of government to Richmond, Virginia, and Congress was to meet there on July 20. The Federal government, meanwhile, with 100,000 Union soldiers camped in and around Washington, decided that now was the time to move. The South had thousands of soldiers camped at Manassas Junction, only twenty-five miles from Washington, and now would be an ideal time to stage that one gigantic battle that would decide the fate of the Union forever. And do it before the Confederate Congress could meet! By July 20 Richmond must be in Union hands!

This force would be led by General Irvin McDowell, a career military man, with some 45,000 troops under his command. They would attack a southern force of some 25,000 troops commanded by General P. G. T. Beauregard, who had ordered the firing on Fort Sumter some three months earlier.

McDowell's plan was to hit the Confederates at their weakly defended position at Bull Run, a small stream near Manassas Junction. But the real success of this venture depended on preventing a Confederate force at Harpers Ferry under General Joseph Johnston from joining the main Confederate Army before or during the fight.

McDowell began moving his army on July 18, and Confederate cavalry immediately informed Beauregard of his movement. Within hours Joe Johnston's brigade was on the long march to Manassas.

McDowell's force struck on Sunday, July 21, and initially the tide seemed to be running in favor of the Union. Indeed, McDowell wired Washington that victory could be expected. But an hour later Johnston's hot and exhausted brigade arrived on the field. At the sight of these robust young southerners, Union forces threw down their muskets and began a retreat that ended in a rout. Yankee congressmen and their lady guests, who were in attendance to observe the Confederacy getting the whipping it deserved, fled in panic, their carriages careening from one hill to the next, all the way back to Washington. (See battle map.)

It was now obvious to Lincoln and the North that the war would not be settled in one day, that it could stretch on for months, or even years. In the South, the prevailing opinion was that the heavily outmanned Confederacy would play a defensive game and wait for the Union to tire of war.

**Ball's Bluff, Virginia, October 21, 1861:** This small engagement proved to be another disaster for the North, costing it 931 casualties and gaining it nothing, except a great deal of embarrassment. Here, a southern brigade, under Colonel Nathan "Shanks" Evans, was holding Leesville, some thirty-five miles up the Potomac from Washington. General George B. McClellan ordered generals Charles Stone and

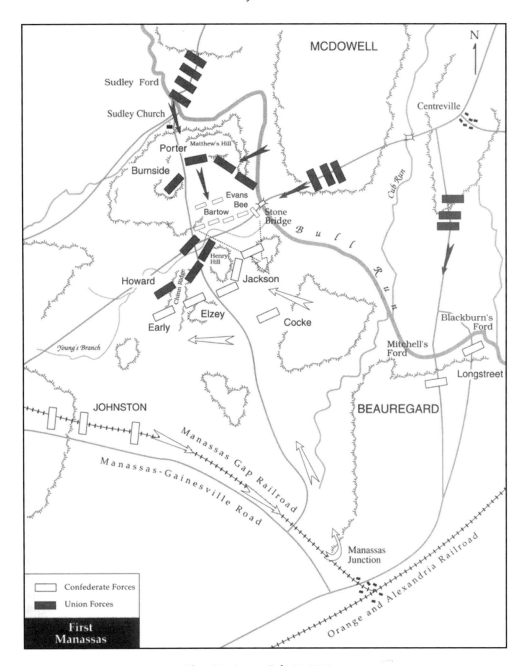

**First Manassas, July 21, 1861.**

George McCall to catch Evans' force in a pincer movement and annihilate them. Unfortunately for the Union, before Stone and McCall could strike the first blow Evans surprised them at Ball's Bluff, and what followed was a Union disaster similar to what had happened at First Manassas. As a result of this engagement, Evans was promoted to brigadier general, while General Stone was accused of treason and arrested without a writ of habeas corpus and thrown into prison for six months.

As 1861 came to a close in Northern Virginia General George B. McClellan was given command of the Union Army, a force of some 200,000 men, concentrated largely in the Washington area, though there were other concentrations in Harpers Ferry; Paducah, Kentucky; and Cairo, Illinois. The Confederate Army, meanwhile, under the command of General Joe Johnston, was largely concentrated southwest of Washington, though smaller units occupied points in northern Tennessee.

## 1861— South and West

**Wilson's Creek (Oak Hills), August 10, 1861:** During the summer of 1861, Confederate troops in the Western Theater were spoiling for a fight. In southwestern Missouri and Arkansas a southern army of about 10,000 troops had been organized under General Sterling Price. To General Nathaniel Lyon, commander of Union forces in Missouri, this Confederate force could not be tolerated. Thus on August 10 Lyon's army of some 7,000 men very rashly attacked the Confederates at Wilson's Creek near Springfield. By day's end the Union men had been thoroughly defeated and Lyon lay dead on the field. (See battle map.)

**Port Royal, South Carolina, November 7, 1861:** Immediately following Fort Sumter, Lincoln proclaimed a blockade of all southern ports. Thus on October 31, Union Flag Officer Samuel F. du Pont led a flotilla of seventeen warships and several transports, carrying some 12,600 troops, to Port Royal, just south of Beaufort, South Carolina. His object was to dismantle the two forts which guarded the entrance to the harbor, Fort Beauregard on Philips Island and Fort Walker on Hilton Head Island. On November 7 the warships entered the harbor in two lines midway between the two forts, bringing all their firepower to bear. The Confederates at that point aban-

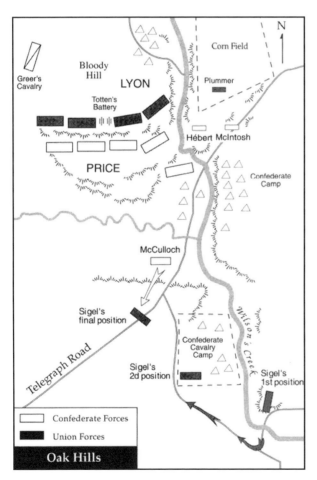

Wilson's Creek (Oak Hills), August 10, 1861.

doned the forts and Union forces were allowed to occupy them unopposed. The loss of Port Royal proved a severe blow to the defense of the southern seaboard, as well as a morale boost for the North which had little to brag about at that point. (See battle map.)

**Columbus, Kentucky, November 15, 1861**: Things in the West remained quiet until November. At that point, General Leonidas Polk, a former Episcopal bishop, commanded a Confederate force at Columbus, at the western tip of Kentucky on the Mississippi River. Union general Ulysses S. Grant was ordered to confront Polk in order to prevent his interfering with the western movement of Union General John C. Frémont. Grant thus ferried 3,000 troops by steamboat to Columbus. There they were met and totally defeated by Polk's brigade. Grant barely escaped with his life.

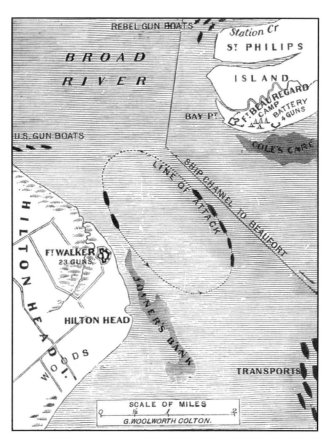

Port Royal, South Carolina, November 7, 1861.

## 1862 — Northern Virginia

**Stonewall Jackson and his Shenandoah Campaign, 1862:** The Shenandoah Valley is bounded on the east by the Blue Ridge Mountains, and on the west by the Alleghenies, and stretches some 165 miles from Lexington to Harpers Ferry. As the war progressed, the Army of Northern Virginia became almost totally dependent on the valley for produce and livestock. Plus, from a geographical standpoint, the valley was a natural doorway into both the North and the South. Soon it became the key to military movements in the Eastern Theater.

By the spring of 1862 the valley became the scene for one of the most brilliant military campaigns in history, one that made Stonewall Jackson famous throughout the western world. In February he established his headquarters at Winchester, twenty-six miles southwest of Harpers Ferry, with a force of 3,600 infantry and 600 cavalry. Soon a Federal army, under General Nathaniel Banks, consisting of some 38,000 soldiers, moved into the Shenandoah. Aware that he was outnumbered ten to one, Jackson

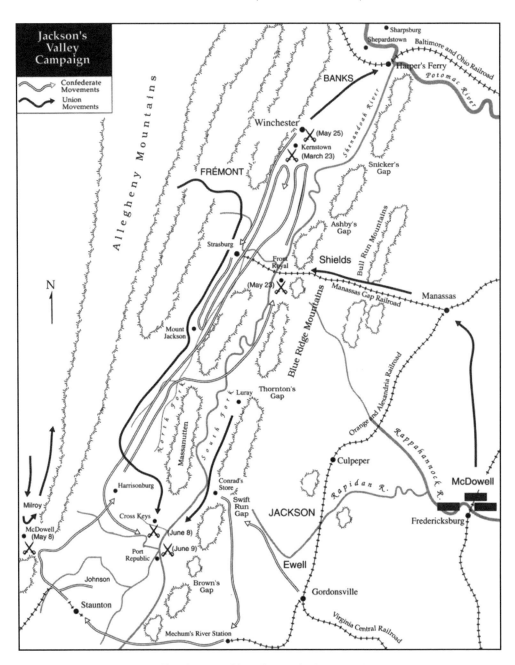

**Jackson's Valley Campaign**

Confederate Movements

Union Movements

Sharpsburg
Shepardstown
Baltimore and Ohio Railroad
Harper's Ferry
Potomac River

BANKS

Winchester
(May 25)
Kernstown
(March 23)
Snicker's Gap

FRÉMONT

Ashby's Gap

Strasburg

Front Royal
Shields

Bull Run Mountains

(May 23)
Manassas Gap Railroad
Manassas

Mount Jackson

Blue Ridge Mountains

Allegheny Mountains

Luray
Thornton's Gap

Massanutten
North Fork
South Fork

Culpeper

Orange and Alexandria Railroad

Rapidan R.

Rappahannock R.

McDowell

N

Harrisonburg
Conrad's Store
Swift Run Gap

JACKSON

Fredericksburg

Milroy
Cross Keys
(June 8)

McDowell
(May 8)
Port Republic
(June 9)

Ewell

Johnson
Brown's Gap

Staunton
Gordonsville

Mechum's River Station
Virginia Central Railroad

Stonewall Jackson and his Shenandoah Campaign, 1862.

began moving his small force northeast, covering forty-one miles in two days, to Kernstown. With barely 2,000 troops at this point, Jackson ordered his exhausted men to attack a full Union division under General James Shields. By nightfall, Jackson was forced to retreat, but he had prevented Shields from reinforcing Union troops at Fredericksburg.

General Robert E. Lee then sent Jackson 8,000 troops under General Richard S. Ewell, and another 2,000 under General Edward Johnson. Leaving Ewell and his men to keep an eye on General Banks, Jackson took his 6,000 men southward. On May 6, after a long march in miserable weather, he arrived at McDowell to confront 4,000 Union troops under General Robert H. Milroy. By evening the Federals were in full retreat.

Jackson then united his force with those of Ewell and Johnson, giving him a total of 17,000 troops. On May 23 he crushed the Union garrison at Front Royal. Then it was on to Winchester, and there on May 25, his men routed General Banks' entire army. In addition to taking over 3,500 prisoners, Jackson's starved soldiers captured such a wealth of quartermaster stores that they began jokingly referring to General Banks as "Commissary Banks."

Jackson's smashing victories had now disrupted the entire Federal offensive in Virginia. On June 9 he defeated a large Union force under General Shields at Port Republic, and the great fight for the Shenandoah Valley was over, at least for a while. Jackson's 17,000 man force had totally defeated 64,000 Union soldiers and three Union generals. (See battle map.)

**Yorktown, Virginia, April and May 1862:** Here McClellan began what has come to be known as his Peninsula Campaign. For two months a force of 15,000 Confed-

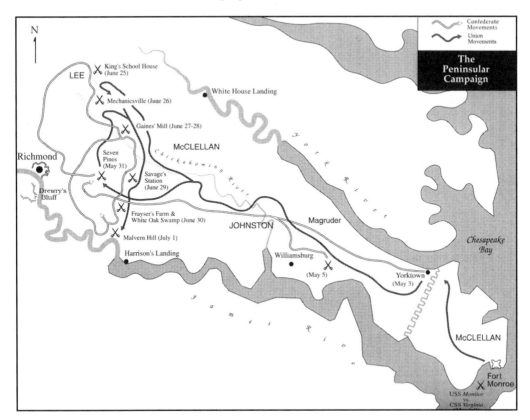

Yorktown, Virginia, April and May 1862.

erates under General John B. Magruder had held McClellan's army of some 100,000 men at bay along defensive lines established near Yorktown, Virginia. McClellan had landed at the tip of the Peninsula in early March with plans to fight his way up to Richmond. But by cleverly shifting his small force from point to point, Magruder fooled McClellan into believing that he was being opposed by a force equal to his own. Thus the timid McClellan began what he called the "siege" of Yorktown. In April General Joe Johnston's forces arrived and immediately Johnston determined that his 56,000 men could not hold the line against McClellan, and thus on May 3–4 the Confederates began a retreat up the Peninsula towards Richmond. (See battle map.)

**Williamsburg, Virginia, May 4–5, 1862:** Following his retreat from Yorktown, General Johnston made a brief stand in a series of earthworks constructed earlier by General Magruder near Williamsburg. This was a rear-guard action intended to allow Johnston's main army to retreat towards Richmond. He left General Lafayette McLaws in charge of this defensive action.

Jeb Stuart's cavalry clashed with McClellan's army giving Johnston the time he needed to make good his escape. Then General James Longstreet's division replaced McLaws' force. The following morning two Union divisions attacked Longstreet who called up reinforcements under General A. P. Hill who immediately recaptured ground lost earlier. By early afternoon, however, their ammunition almost depleted, Hill was forced to pull back. General Johnston then arrived on the scene and ordered General D. H. Hill's division to support Longstreet. Hill then ordered General Jubal Early's brigade to immediately attack General Hancock's Union force. Too eager to comply, Early brought up only two of his four regiments and though they were initially successful, they were eventually beaten back. With nightfall, having suffered some 1,500 casualties, the Confederates withdrew from this hard-fought engagement and continued their retreat towards Richmond.

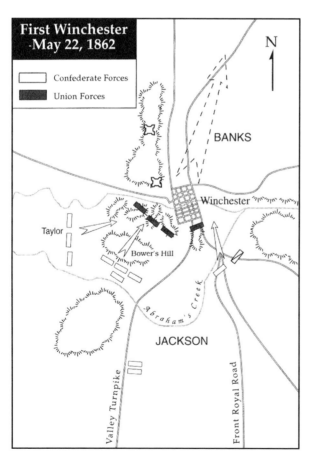

First Battle of Winchester, May 25, 1862.

**The First Battle of Winchester, May 25, 1862:** The first battle of Winchester occurred on June 25, 1862, following Stonewall Jackson's defeat of Union forces at Front Royal only two days earlier. Here, Jackson, with 17,000 Confederates, divided his force into two groups, one along the Front Royal road to the southeast and the main attack column on the Valley Turnpike to the southwest.

Those along the Valley Turnpike were to take the high ground in that area in order to dislodge some 8,000 Union soldiers atop Bowers Hill under General Nathaniel P. Banks. Almost immediately Union artillery began to rain shells down on the Confederates only four hundred yards to their front, inflicting heavy casualties. Thus Jackson ordered General Richard Taylor to flank the enemy's left flank. Two hours later, while Jackson's main force kept the attention of the Federals, Taylor and his infantry swept the surprised Federals from the high ground

By sundown Banks and his Federals were in retreat, and did not pause until after they had crossed the Potomac. Even so, Banks lost over half his force, with some 3,000 captured. Jackson lost only 400 men. More importantly, this action halted the advance of 40,000 Union troops to the peninsula where Gen. McClelland threatened Richmond. (See battle map.)

**Fair Oaks, Virginia (Seven Pines) May 31, 1862:** Less than six miles from Richmond, McClellan won a victory here against Joe Johnston but failed to take advantage of it. General Johnston, in fact, had devised a very clever battle plan at Fair Oaks, with General James Longstreet leading the attack, but a series of unlikely miscom-

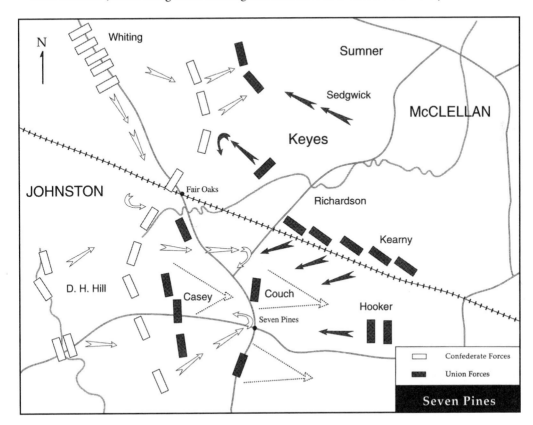

Fair Oaks, Virginia (Seven Pines), May 31, 1862.

munications spelled doom for the attack, and the Federals won the day. Late in the afternoon Johnston was seriously wounded in this engagement and command of the Confederate Army passed to General Gustavus V. Smith, second in command to Johnston, but an exhausted Smith requested that he be relieved of command. Thus command of the Army of Northern Virginia passed to General Robert E. Lee. (See battle map.)

**Stuart's Ride Around McClellan, June 12–15, 1862:** General Jeb Stuart's most famous expedition occurred on June 12–15 during the Peninsula campaign. In order to carry out his plans to relieve Union pressure on Richmond, General Lee ordered

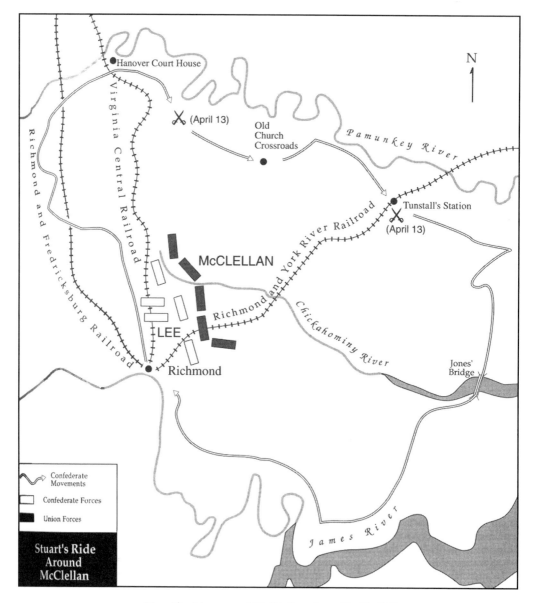

Stuart's ride around McClellan, June 12–15, 1862.

Stuart "to make a secret movement to the rear of the enemy" to determine the practicality of striking the Union army's right wing north of the Chickahominy River. Thus on the morning of June 12 Stuart led 1,200 men of his cavalry troop on the long ride to Hanover Court House, to the north of Richmond. The following day, June 13, he changed directions, heading east to the Old Church Crossroads. To date, except for a brief exchange with elements of the Fifth U.S. Cavalry, Stuart had met with no opposition. (It was in this engagement that Captain William Latane of the Ninth Virginia Cavalry was killed.)

He arrived at Old Church on the afternoon of June 13. So far Stuart's semicircular route had carried him thirty-five miles from Richmond and behind Gen. McClelland's army. He had discovered that McClellan's right flank was indeed vulnerable, and he became concerned about his own rear, fearing that the Federals would intercept his return home. He thus decided upon "the quintessence of prudence," and turned his cavalry south in an attempt to ride completely around McClelland's army. He would later inform Lee: "There was something of the sublime in the implicit confidence and unquestioning trust of the rank and file in a leader guiding them straight into the very jaws of the enemy." (No one could accuse Stuart of being overly modest.)

On this leg of his journey Stuart seized and burned supply wagons and nearly captured a train. On June 14 they reached the banks of the Chickahominy but could not cross the rain-swollen river. Stuart simply designed and constructed a bridge, which allowed his horsemen to cross over. And just in time, for by now he was being closely pursued by his father-in-law, Gen. Philip St. George Cooke, and his cavalry brigade.

Stuart returned to Richmond on June 15 after nearly a hundred miles of riding. He returned with 165 prisoners and 260 captured horses, plus the news that McClelland's right flank was indeed vulnerable. (See battle map.)

**Seven Days' Battles, June 25–July 1, 1862:** These battles constituted the end of McClellan's Peninsula Campaign which carried the Army of the Potomac to within seven miles of Richmond. General Lee, who had been waiting for a chance to seize the initiative, received that chance when Jeb Stuart, who had ridden completely around McClellan's army, reported that the Union right flank, a force of some 30,000 men commanded by General Fitz-John Porter, was separated from the Union's main force and vulnerable to attack. Lee thus sent the majority of his army, bolstered by General Stonewall Jackson's brigade called in from the Shenandoah Valley, to annihilate McClellan's army in one decisive battle. (See battle map.)

**Oak Grove, June 25, 1862:** General Jackson, supported by divisions under generals A. P. Hill, James Longstreet, and D. H. Hill, began the attack before everyone was in position. As a result, Porter's men repulsed attack after attack. It was a defeat that cost the South 1,484 casualties.

**Gaines' Mill, June 26, 1862:** Again, Porter's men repulsed repeated assaults from Confederate forces until the southerners retired for the day. Still, despite even more casualties, Lee pressed on, hoping to annihilate McClellan's army in one decisive battle.

**Savage's Station, June 29, Frayser's Farm, June 30, Malvern Hill, July 1, and Mechanicsville, July 2, 1862:** Although this series of battles failed to destroy McClel-

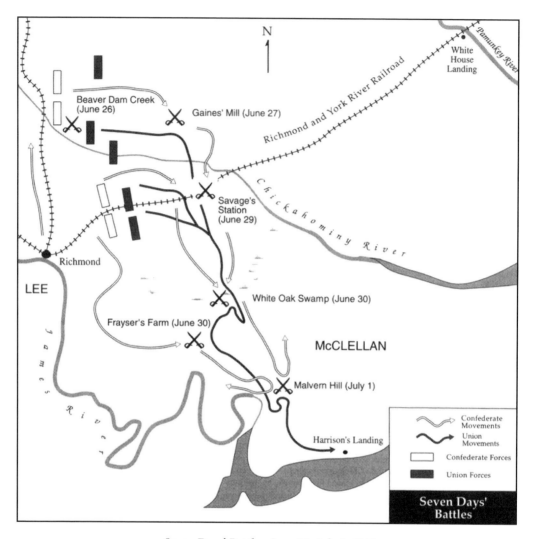

Seven Days' Battles, June 25–July 2, 1862.

lan's army, as Lee had planned to do, they did indeed force the Federals from the gates of Richmond, and they also established for Lee a reputation for boldness and ingenuity. But it came at a great price to the Confederacy as the southerners suffered some 20,000 casualties in these seven engagements. Still, the Federals had been driven thirty miles away from Richmond.

**Second Manassas (Bull Run), August 29–September 1, 1862:** Lee now wanted to strike Pope's main army before it could be reinforced by McClellan's Army of the Peninsula. Thus he sent Stonewall Jackson and Jeb Stuart around Pope's right flank to destroy the Federal supply depot at Manassas Junction. They succeeded in their mission, and Pope, now totally frightened that he had an enemy army between himself and Washington, began to retreat towards the capital. Lee brought his scattered army together at Manassas on August 29. After two days of fighting, the thoroughly defeated Pope continued his retreat. But on September 1 Lee again caught up with the timid Pope at Chantilly and inflicted heavy casualties.

The Union lost 16,000 men in these engagements, the South 9,000. (See battle map.)

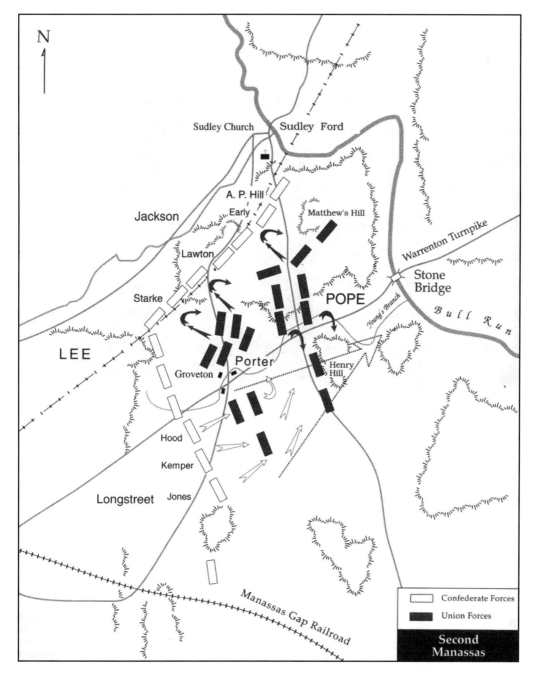

The Second Manassas (Bull Run), August 29–September 1, 1862.

**Cedar Mountain, August 9, 1862**: General Lee was eager to test General Pope and his Army of Virginia, and thus he ordered Stonewall Jackson to attack a Union force under General Nathaniel Banks before it could join Pope's main army at Culpeper. Banks became aware that he was being pursued by Jackson, and on August 9 he turned and attacked Jackson at Cedar Mountain. Banks was soundly defeated.

**Sharpsburg (Antietam), Maryland, September 17, 1862**: In early September General Lee decided the time was ripe to invade Maryland. He hoped to inflict another wound upon the Army of the Potomac before winter set in, and to gather food and forage from the fertile fields of that great state. General McClellan, by a stroke of good luck, found Lee's Special Order 191, outlining his plan of attack, though he failed to exploit the find. On September 14, Lee's small army suffered a defeat at South Mountain. It was a minor engagement, but it convinced Lee to retreat to Virginia. It was at Sharpsburg on his return march on September 17 that the two armies met at Antietam Creek. By this time the divisions of Stonewall Jackson, Richard Ewell, John Walker, and Lafayette McLaws had arrived from Harpers Ferry, giving Lee a force of some 35,000 men. Still, he was outnumbered three to one. Following a terrible daylong fight, with the dead and wounded carpeting the fields, neither side could claim a clear victory. Then in the late afternoon, just when it appeared that Union soldiers would totally overwhelm the outnumbered Confederates, General A. P. Hill's division arrived after a seventeen-mile march from Harpers Ferry. Immediately his exhausted soldiers charged General Burnside's left flank, and the startled Union soldiers broke and ran, saving Lee's army from annihilation. This engagement has been called the bloodiest single day in American military history, with the Union suffering 12,410 casualties, the South 13,724. Despite his heavy losses, Lee again challenged McClellan on the morning of the eighteenth, but McClellan refused to fight, and thus that afternoon the Army of Northern Virginia, having won a great victory against overwhelming odds, turned south. (See battle map.)

**Harpers Ferry, Virginia, September 13–15, 1862**: In this three-day fight General Stonewall Jackson's men captured 12,500 Union prisoners (the largest surrender of Federal troops during the entire war), and enabled Robert E. Lee to cease his withdrawal from Maryland and to fight the Battle of Antietam on September 17.

While camped at Frederick, Maryland, Lee became concerned about the 14,000 Federals at Harpers Ferry, blocking his access to vital supply lines into the Shenandoah Valley. Thus on September 9 he issued Special Order 191, a strategic move designed to eliminate the Union garrisons in the lower valley. Special Order 191 divided his army into four parts. Three columns, comprising six divisions and totaling 23,000 men, would march upon Harpers Ferry from three directions, seize the three mountains surrounding the town, and thus trap the Federals between the hills. Lee and the remainder of his army, meanwhile, would await the return of these divisions at Boonsboro, Maryland, twenty miles north of Harpers Ferry. Lee selected General Stonewall Jackson to direct the attack on Harpers Ferry, and he had only three days to accomplish his mission.

On the morning of September 10 General John G. Walker and his two thousand men began their march to Loudoun Heights, a steep bluff overlooking Harper's Ferry from the south bank of the Shenandoah River. General Lafayette McLaws and his seven thousand troops, along with General Richard Anderson's division, began making their way to Maryland Heights, the high ridge overlooking Harpers Ferry from north of the Potomac. Stonewall Jackson, meanwhile, with fourteen thousand men from his own division and the divisions of General Richard Ewell and General A. P. Hill,

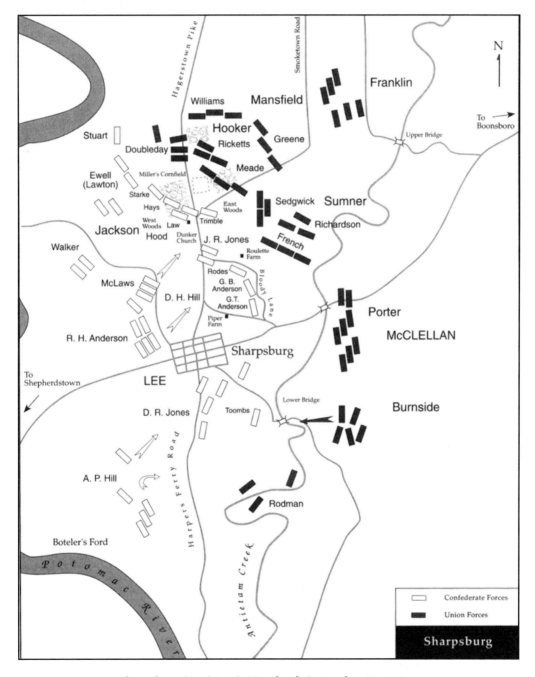

Sharpsburg (Antietam), Maryland, September 17, 1862.

marched hurriedly to Martinsburg, and there these poor emaciated, barefoot southerners frightened the Union garrison into a hasty retreat to Harpers Ferry.

Colonel Dixon Miles, commander of Federal troops at Harpers Ferry, knew the southerners were coming and mistakenly believed that Bolivar Heights would be the point of their attack. Thus he placed the bulk of his garrison of 10,000 men atop Bolivar Heights. Nor did Miles believe that the Confederates could drag their long range cannon a thousand feet to the crest of Maryland and Loudoun Heights. Thus he assigned only 2,000 men to defend these two hills.

Miles' miscalculations proved fortunate for Jackson's men, already slowed by swollen rivers and a lack of shoes and very little food. Still, they covered 51 miles in only 72 hours.

Special Order 191 stipulated that Harpers Ferry must be captured by September 12. That day arrived and Jackson's men had still not reached their target. Their situation was further complicated the following day when McClellan was given a copy of Special Order 191. He immediately (and prematurely) boasted that he had "all the plans of the Rebels and would catch them in their own trap."

Finally, on September 13 General Walker's men occupied Loudoun Heights without firing a shot. General Jackson's 14,000 men blocked escape from the west by settling upon School House Ridge, which paralleled the main Federal position on Bolivar Heights. The brigades of General Joseph Kershaw and William Barksdale, both of McLaw's command, drove the Federals from Maryland Heights after a six hour battle. By dusk of September 13 Confederate forces completely surrounded Harpers Ferry.

At that point General Miles informed General McClelland of his predicament and requested help. McClelland responded the next day by attacking three gaps in South Mountain to "cut the enemy in two and beat him in detail." The Confederates beat back these incursion, however, thus giving Jackson one more day to conquer Harpers Ferry.

To that end, Jackson ordered his cannon atop Loudoun Heights to begin shelling Federal positions where Federal troops had sought refuge. He also ordered A. P. Hill's 3,000 troops to flank the Union left on Bolivar Heights .

With his garrison now outflanked and outgunned, Colonel Miles surrendered on the morning of September 15. Jackson captured 73 pieces of artillery, 13,000 small arms, 200 wagons, and 12,500 prisoners. Jackson lost 39 killed and 247 wounded. He rejoined Lee's army on September 16.

**Fredericksburg, December 13, 1862:** General Burnside, who had twice refused command of the Army of the Potomac, was given the job following the Battle of Sharpsburg. Immediately, he laid plans to cross the Rappahannock, capture Fredericksburg, and then move on Richmond. By December 10, when he finally received the pontoons necessary to cross the Rappahannock, the forces of both General Longstreet and Stonewall Jackson had joined Lee and occupied the heights north and south of the town. The divisions of D. H. Hill and Jubal Early were being held in reserve. On December 12, after Burnside's artillery had reduced Fredericksburg to rubble, Union soldiers entered the city and devoted the rest of the day to pillaging and stealing whatever they could find, much to the chagrin of Union officers. The following day, December 13, Burnside ordered his 115,000-man army to charge Lee's 80,000-man force. Charge after charge was thrown at the Confederates, but they were repeatedly repulsed. By nightfall Union dead littered the fields, and all for naught. The next day, having lost some 13,000 men, what was left of Burnside's forces recrossed the Rappahannock to lick its wounds. It has been said that the Army of the Potomac never suffered a more costly or humiliating defeat. As for the Army of Northern Virginia, it experienced perhaps its easiest triumph of the war. (See battle map.)

## 1862 — South and West

**Forts Henry and Donelson, Tennessee, February 6–14, 1862:** By the first of the year General Grant, headquartered at Paducah, Kentucky, felt that he could break the Confederate line that stretched across northern Tennessee and southern Kentucky by capturing forts Henry and Donelson. Fort Henry stood on the Tennessee River just south of the Kentucky border, while Donelson was on the Cumberland River some twelve miles to the east. General Joe Johnston's poorly trained and equipped Army of Tennessee stood little chance of repelling such an attack. And indeed when Union naval

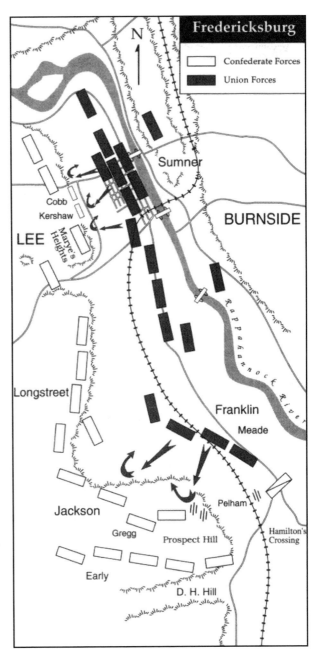

Fredericksburg, Virginia, December 13, 1862.

and land forces struck Fort Henry on February 6, the southern boys fled to Fort Donelson without firing a shot. As a result, Union forces now controlled the Tennessee River, thus forcing General Johnston to abandon his position at Bowling Green.

Johnston immediately dispatched generals John B. Floyd, Gideon Pillow, Simon Bolivar Buckner, and Bushrod Rust Johnson, along with 18,000 soldiers, to defend

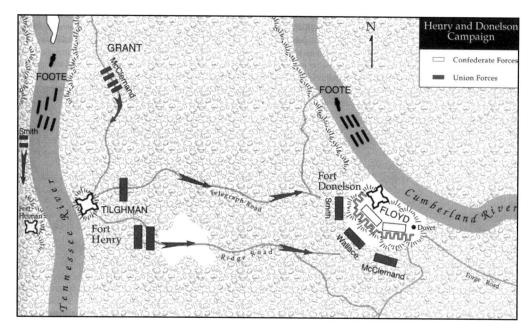

Forts Henry and Donelson, Tennessee, February 6–14, 1862.

Fort Donelson. Their mission was to hold the fort (and Grant's army) long enough for Johnston to move his Army of Central Kentucky southward to Nashville.

The battle for Donelson began on February 13, and the first day of fighting was won by the southerners, who repulsed every Union advance. The next morning Confederate artillery, located on the high bluffs guarding Donelson, defeated a large force of Union ironclads. Still, the four generals in command of Donelson saw the grim writing on the wall and decided to escape the trap they now faced.

At dawn Pillow's and Buckner's divisions fought their way through a large Union force blocking the road to Nashville and freedom. For whatever reason, they failed to take advantage of it and returned to the fort. Then the four generals began an argument that lasted throughout the night. Finally, they decided to surrender to Grant at dawn. At that point Colonel Nathan Bedford Forrest told them "to go to hell," that he was not surrendering to anybody, and stomped angrily from the room. In the end, generals Floyd, Pillow, Forrest and Johnson managed to escape with their troops to Nashville, leaving Buckner to surrender the fort to Grant. (See battle map.)

**Elkhorn Tavern (Pea Ridge), Arkansas, March 7–8, 1862:** In 1861 General Sterling Price had been unable to hold Lexington and thus retreated to the southwest corner of Missouri where he established a base at Springfield. Since that time the War Department had established the Trans-Mississippi District with General Earl Van Dorn in command of the Army of the Southwest. Van Dorn arrived in Arkansas on March 2 and began making plans to reinforce Price and General Ben McCulloch for an invasion of Missouri and the capture of St. Louis. To meet that threat Union general Samuel R. Curtis moved south from Rolla with 10,250 men. Van Dorn then divided his 16,500-man force into two divisions. Also, Price still had his Missouri force and McCulloch commanded two brigades of Texas, Arkansas and Louisiana troops. In addition General Stand Watie and his Indians from the five southern tribes were called in from the Indian Territory (Oklahoma).

General Curtis' line ran near an inn known as Elkhorn Tavern, three miles south of a high plateau called Pea Ridge, in an area well protected from the south. Van Dorn thus decided to attack Curtis from the rear. But Curtis had not been fooled. On the morning of March 7, he met the forces of Price and McCulloch head on. As though things were not already bad enough, McCulloch was killed early that afternoon. Van Dorn's men then joined Price at Pea Ridge. By nightfall Confederate forces had driven the Federals in retreat from Elkhorn Tavern and victory seemed assured. The following morning, his force now reinforced by McCulloch's men, Van Dorn formed a defensive line near Elkhorn Tavern. But the southerners, as so often happened, soon ran short of ammunition. Thus it was necessary that they retreat as quickly as possible, turning victory into defeat. The South suffered about 1,500 casualties in this engagement, the North about the same.

This defeat insured that the Federals would maintain control of Missouri. As for Van Dorn, who did not adapt well to the situation at Elkhorn Tavern, his army was transferred to the east side of the Mississippi at the end of March, and the Trans-Mississippi Department was relegated to a minor position for the rest of the war. (See battle map.)

**Pittsburg Landing (Shiloh), April 6–7, 1862:** In March of '62 the Confederate War Department ordered that some 40,000 men be concentrated at Corinth, Mississippi, under the command of General Albert Sidney Johnston. It was his mission to crush General Grant at Pittsburgh Landing (twenty-two miles north of

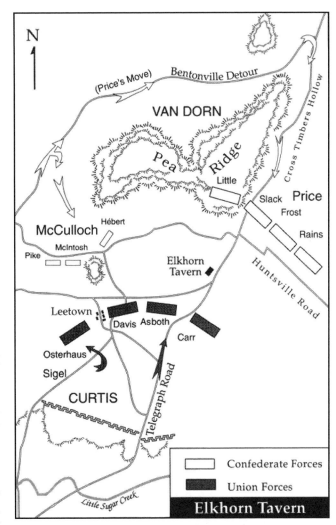

Elkhorn Tavern (Pea Ridge), Arkansas, March 7–8, 1862.

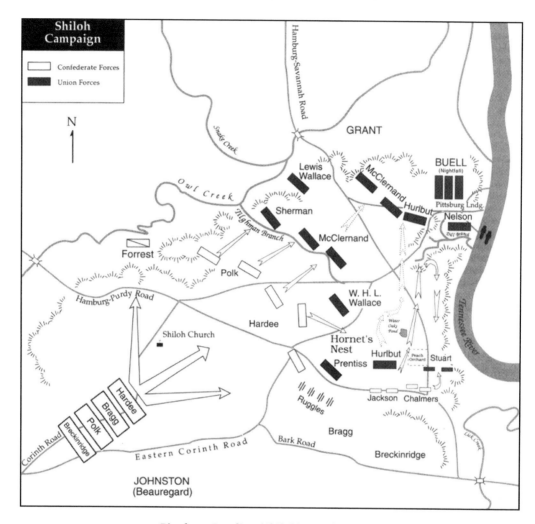

Pittsburg Landing (Shiloh), April 6–7, 1862.

Corinth) before he could be reinforced. Thus, at dawn on Sunday, April 6, the Confederates struck a totally surprised Union army.

Later that afternoon General Johnston was killed and command was passed to General P. G. T. Beauregard, hero of First Manassas. The South had won the day, but Beauregard was unaware of just how decisive the victory really was, and thus he ordered that the attack be suspended. By nightfall Grant's reinforcements arrived and began an attack on Confederate lines at daybreak. By 6 P.M. Confederate forces were in full retreat towards Corinth. A great victory had been squandered, and at a terrible cost: the South lost 10,000 men in this engagement, Grant 13,000. Also, as a result of this defeat, the South lost Corinth and then Memphis and the rest of western Tennessee. (See battle map.)

**New Madrid and Island Number 10, Missouri, March–April, 1862:** General Polk sent General John Porter McCown with 5,000 men to reinforce the 2,000 troops already manning the forts at New Madrid and Island Number 10 (ten miles upriver from New Madrid). These were the Confederacy's uppermost outposts on the Mississippi River and essential to the South's controlling the river. On March 13, General John Pope's 18,000-man force, supported by six Union gunboats, began a bombardment of New Madrid, convincing McCown to transfer his garrison from the fort to the peninsula across the river in order to avoid being trapped.

This decision cost McCown his command and he was replaced on March 31 by General William W. Mackall. Following a terrible engagement led by the Union gunboats which shelled the Confederates night and day, Mackall surrendered his 7,000 men to General Pope on April 8. It was this engagement that convinced Lincoln to name Pope commander of the Army of Virginia.

**Fort Pulaski, Georgia, April 10–11, 1862:** Constructed by Robert E. Lee in 1847 and seized by the Georgia Militia on January 6, 1861, Ft. Pulaski fell to Union forces on April 11, 1862, thus eliminating Savannah as a badly needed blockade-running seaport for the Confederacy.

The previous November Union forces under Captain Quincy A. Gillmore had landed on nearby Typee Island with plans to bombard Pulaski into submission. To that end, the Federals erected 11 batteries containing 36 heavy guns and mortars at ranges varying between 1,650 and 3,400 yards. Ft. Pulaski, on the other hand, could answer with 48 cannons and 385 officers and men, all under the command of Col. Charles Olmstead.

The Federals opened fire on Pulaski on the morning of April 10, and by evening a breach was plainly visible in the southeast wall. Olmstead recognized the danger, but incoming fire throughout the night hampered repair efforts. The following morning the breach had become so wide that Federal gunners could aim shells through it and across the parade ground towards the fort magazine. Now, with 16 cannon dismounted and his garrison endangered by the possible explosion of 40,000 pounds of gunpowder, Olmstead at 2:00 P.M. hoisted a bedsheet and Gillmore rowed over to receive a formal surrender.

During this two-day bombardment 5,175 shot and shell had been fired against Ft. Pulaski, but the breach was caused almost entirely by three large rifled cannon, leading artillerists to predict that rifled cannon would revolutionize such warfare.

**Iuka, Mississippi, September 1, 1862:** Twenty-two miles east of Corinth, on the Memphis and Charleston railway, Iuka was now occupied by a Confederate corps under General Sterling Price. General Grant thus dispatched Rosecrans' two divisions to attack Price from the south, while General E. O. C. Ord moved out of Corinth with 8,000 men to attack Price from the west. Price, however, was not surprised by this move, and instead of suffering a surprise attack, he immediately seized the offensive and drove the enemy back on all fronts during the day's fight. The following day, badly outnumbered, Price withdrew his force and joined General Earl Van Dorn for his attack on Corinth. Nearly 800 Union troops were lost in this engagement; the South lost twice that number.

**Munfordville, Kentucky, September 13–17, 1862:** Located thirty-five miles northeast of Bowling Green, on the Green River, Munfordville was a center for the

Louisville and Nashville Railroad. On September 10 it was garrisoned on both sides of the river by some 4,000 Union troops under Colonel John T. Wilder.

In August, Braxton Bragg with 30,000 troops in Chattanooga and Kirby Smith with 10,000 troops in Knoxville began an invasion of Kentucky in order to secure that state for the Confederacy. By September 13, though pursued by Don Carlos Buell's 55,000 troops, Kirby Smith had occupied Frankfort and Bragg was moving in the direction of Munfordville.

That same day, Bragg ordered a brigade of Mississippi troops under General James Ronald Chalmers to force Colonel Wilder to surrender the city. Wilder refused, and Chalmers ordered his men to attack. Their attack was beaten back, but again Chalmers demanded the surrender of the city. Again Wilder refused.

On September 16 Bragg brought his entire army to bear upon Wilder's forces and planned an immediate attack, with William J. Hardee and Leonidas Polk surrounding the town. But General Simon Bolivar Buckner, worried about the safety of many of his friends who lived in the city, pleaded with Bragg to postpone his action. Buckner then conducted Colonel Wilder on a tour of Confederate positions. Convinced finally that his force had no chance, Wilder surrendered the garrison on the morning of September 17.

Corinth, Mississippi, October 3–4, 1862.

**Corinth, Mississippi, October 3–4, 1862:** Following General Bragg's decision to launch his Kentucky campaign, Bragg departed Mississippi, leaving behind two independent southern forces. One, a force of some 7,000 men, was commanded by General Earl Van Dorn, the other, a force of some 17,000 men, by General Sterling Price. Price's forces were commanded by General Dabney H. Maury and General Louis Hebert. Van

Dorn had no authority over Price unless their forces were united, which was fortunate since Price loathed Van Dorn. At the end of September Bragg ordered Van Dorn and Price to attack and dislodge General Rosecrans' troops from the area of Corinth. On October 3 Van Dorn's men pushed Rosecrans' divisions back for several miles, but at that point, hungry, thirsty, exhausted and running low on ammunition, they were forced to suspend operations for the day. On the morning of the fourth, after sharp fighting throughout the day the arrival of Federal reinforcements convinced Van Dorn to withdraw to the safety of Holly Springs. The South suffered 4,800 casualties in this fight, while the North lost a total of 2,400. (See battle map.)

**Chaplin Hills (Perryville), Kentucky, October 8, 1862:** General Braxton Bragg assumed command of the Army of the West following Beauregard's unauthorized sick leave, and immediately launched his Kentucky campaign. In early September he led his army to Munfordville, Kentucky, where he easily defeated a Union force of 4,000 troops. On September 17, wishing to confer with General Kirby Smith, Bragg traveled to Lexington, Kentucky, leaving his army of 48,000 men under the command of General Leonidas Polk. Two weeks later Polk moved the army to Perryville in order to meet a threat from Union general Don Carlos Buell's army of 61,000. Polk was soon joined by the forces of generals William Hardee, Simon Bolivar Buckner, Bushrod Rust Johnson and a cavalry brigade under Colonel Joe Wheeler. Following faulty planning and a series of indecisive moves by Polk, a frustrated Bragg arrived back in Perryville on October 8. The Confederates then pushed Buell back two miles before the advance stalled. Though Bragg was not defeated in this battle, his army suffered 3,100 casualties, about 20 percent of the Confederates involved. That evening he began a retreat that ended in Tennessee. (See battle map.)

**Holly Springs, Mississippi, December 20, 1862:** Located thirty-five miles southeast of Memphis, Holly Springs was the site of a raid by Earl Van Dorn which forced General Ulysses S. Grant to postpone his drive to capture Vicksburg, and cost the Federals some 1,500 men captured and $1,500,000 in destroyed supplies.

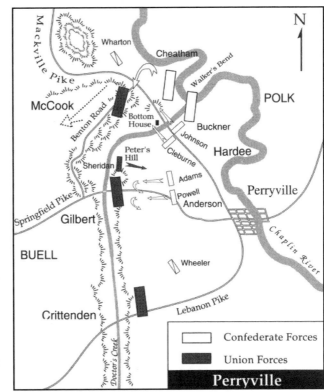

Chaplin Hills (Perryville), Kentucky, October 8, 1862.

On December 12, 1862 at his headquarters in Grenada, Mississippi, General John C. Pemberton concentrated his various cavalry brigades under the command of General Earl Van Dorn in order to raid General Grant's supply base at Holly Springs. Van Dorn thus took charge of Colonel John Griffith's Sixth, Ninth, and Twenty-Seventh Texas Cavalry brigades, plus Colonel William H. Jackson's Mississippi and Tennessee Cavalry, and Colonel Robert McCulloch's First Mississippi and Second Missouri Cavalry, a total force of some 3,500 men.

Van Dorn swore his three brigade commanders to secrecy concerning their destination, and then they, knowing they faced a long and grueling ride, began weeding out those cavalrymen who would not be able to keep pace.

On the morning of December 17, the southerners began their long ride, avoiding any roads that led to Holly Springs in hopes that the Federals would be fooled into believing that his force was bound for Tennessee. On the evening of December 18, near Ripley, Van Dorn and his men rested and fed their horses. Guards were posted at every farm house to insure that no one informed the Federals that a raiding party was on their way. At sunrise on December 20, Van Dorn ordered Colonel Griffith and his Texas Cavalry Brigades to enter Holly Springs from the west. McCulloch's men were to enter from the south, and Jackson's men were to enter from the north.

By this time the Union commander at Holly Springs, Colonel Robert C. Murphy, was aware that the Confederates were nearby, and tried to alert the garrisons at the north and south ends of town, and he set his infantry to work building barricades out of bales of cotton. But he was too late.

Griffith's Texans captured Union pickets without firing a shot, then went on and captured the railway depot and its defenders, among them Colonel Murphy. McCulloch's First Mississippi, after a hard fight, captured the fairgrounds where the Union cavalry camped. Then came the First Missouri to the fairgrounds where they mopped up remnants of the 101st Illinois.

Holly Springs was now in Confederate hands. (General Grant's wife, General James Longstreet's first cousin, was in town during the fight but was closely protected and not harmed.)

The destruction of the Holly Springs supply base, along with Nathan Bedford Forrest's raids in western Tennessee, forced Grant to postpone his advance on Vicksburg for six months. (See battle map.)

Holly Springs, Mississippi, December 20, 1862.

**Chickasaw Bluffs, Mississippi, December 26–28, 1862:** In a strong effort to capture Vicksburg, General Grant sent General William Tecumseh Sherman with a force of 32,000 men to capture Chickasaw Bayou, the city's northernmost defense line. But the southerners, under General Stephen Dill Lee, thoroughly smashed Sherman's troops and turned this three-day battle into a Union disaster. Sherman immediately withdrew the remainder of his force.

**Murfreesboro, Tennessee, December 31–January 2, 1862–63:** Rosecrans, in an effort to capture Murfreesboro and annihilate General Braxton Bragg's army of 37,700 in the process, began his offensive at Stones River on the morning of December 31. In a cleverly planned defense, Bragg immediately assumed the offensive. He assigned William J. Hardee to hit the Union right flank, while Leonidas Polk's force would hit the Union center. General John C. Breckinridge's division was initially held in reserve, though it would later be nearly destroyed in a series of fruitless charges. (Breckinridge threatened to shoot Bragg as a result.) By nightfall of the first day's fighting, Bragg was convinced that the South had won a great victory. But the following morning he learned that Rosecrans intended to stand and fight. He also learned of his terrible losses. The following day Bragg ordered Breckinridge to strike the Union line with his full force, and for a while it looked as though he might succeed. But then Union reinforcements arrived and Breckinridge's men were decimated. Despite the heroic fighting on the part of Confederate troops, it was obvious by nightfall of the third day that the South could no longer hold Murfreesboro. Bragg thus withdrew his Army of Tennessee to Shelbyville. The South lost 9,870 men in this engagement, the North 12,700. Bragg won a tactical victory here, but it was hardly worth the cost. (See battle map.)

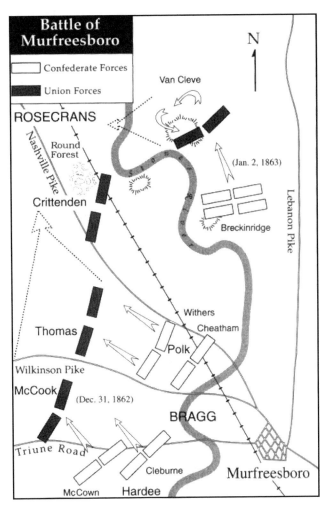

Murfreesboro, Tennessee, December 31–January 2, 1862–63.

## 1863 — Northern Virginia and Pennsylvania

**Chancellorsville, Virginia, May 1–3, 1863:** On January 25, 1863, a desperate Abe Lincoln replaced Burnside as commander of the Army of the Potomac with General Joseph Hooker. With the advent of spring, Hooker was eager to show what he could do. Thus on May 1, trying to avoid the mistakes Burnside had made earlier, he moved his army southward in a second attempt to take Fredericksburg. Hooker left a third of his force in front of General Lee's entrenchments, moving the rest to the west in a wide sweep around Lee's left flank. Lee left General Jubal Early's men to face the Federals while moving his main force west to meet Hooker. The battle began on May 1, Hooker's 134,000 men opposing Lee's 60,000. But instead of waiting to be attacked, Lee's men audaciously charged Hooker's advancing force, and the first day of fighting ended in a stalemate.

That night Lee and Stonewall Jackson planned a new strategy. Despite being outnumbered by more than two to one, at dawn Jackson with 26,000 men attacked Hooker's right flank, which collapsed after a brutal day of fighting. Then as evening set in, Jackson's men hit Hooker's left flank. Almost immediately the Federals threw down their rifles and fled in panic. A complete rout would have ensued except for a terrible misfortune. Stonewall Jackson, riding ahead of his attacking line, was mistakenly

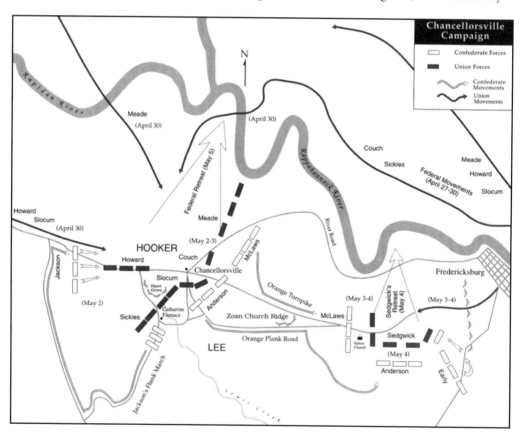

Chancellorsville, Virginia, May 1–3, 1863.

fired on by men of the Eighteenth North Carolina Regiment and received three terrible wounds. His arm was amputated on May 3, and on May 10 he died of pneumonia at Guiney Station. The death of Stonewall Jackson was one of the worst disasters to befall the South during the war.

Following a third day of fighting, Hooker admitted defeat and withdrew his army across the Rappahannock River. Again, a badly outnumbered South had won a resounding victory over a poorly led, poorly motivated Union army, and again at a terrible price. The Confederacy lost 13,000 men, the North 18,000. (See battle map.)

**Gettysburg, Pennsylvania, July 1–3, 1863:** To date the Union army had suffered horrendous casualties in the war, and anti-war sentiment was growing by leaps and bounds in the north. Hoping to exploit this sentiment, and encouraged by his recent great victory at Chancellorsville, General Lee decided to move his Army of Northern Virginia into Maryland and Pennsylvania and hopefully inflict a defeat upon the Army of the Potomac. His goal was the capture of Harrisburg, the capital of Pennsylvania, thus adding to the problems faced by the Lincoln administration. He also hoped that a Confederate victory would encourage England and France to recognize the South.

Lee organized his army into three corps of 20,000 men each. General James Longstreet commanded the First Corps; Richard Ewell the Second (Stonewall Jackson's old corps); and A. P. Hill the Third. General Jeb Stuart commanded Lee's cavalry division. In all, Lee led a force of 75,000 men into Pennsylvania. They moved northwest from Fredericksburg on June 3. General Hooker, aware that Lee's army was on the march, began moving his Army of the Potomac on a parallel course. Three weeks later, with Lee now in Pennsylvania, Hooker suddenly resigned his commission, and was replaced by General George Meade.

The Confederates fought several engagements along their way to Gettysburg:

**Brandy Station, Virginia, June 10, 1863:** Almost immediately, Stuart was attacked at Brandy Station by a Union cavalry force of 11,000 men under General Alfred Pleasonton. After recovering from his initial shock at having allowed himself to be ambushed by 11,000 Federal horsemen, Stuart inflicted heavy casualties on Pleasonton's cavalry, forcing their hasty retreat. Brandy Station was the largest cavalry battle of the entire war.

**The Second Winchester, June 14, 1863:** In the vanguard of General Lee's assault into Pennsylvania, General Richard Ewell, commander of Lee's Second Corps, saw an opportunity to liberate Winchester, then under the control of General Robert H. Milroy and his 7,000 Federal infantry, and avoid future communication problems for Lee's army once they reached Pennsylvania. On the afternoon of June 14 Ewell's corps took up positions around Winchester. Ewell ordered, General Jubal Early to attack from the west, while General Johnson's men were to lie in wait. Shortly after six that afternoon Confederate artillery commenced a crushing fire on the Federals. Then came a charge by Early's Virginians that succeeded in routing Milroy's Union defenders. Several hours later, just after midnight, Milroy attempted to escape with what remained of his force, but their escape was cut off by General Johnson near Stephenson's Depot, four miles from Winchester. In only several hours the Federals lost 4,443 men, while Ewell lost but 269.

**Confederate Military Departments, June 30, 1863.**

On June 15 leading elements of Lee's army entered Pennsylvania. As for Jeb Stuart, he had circled behind the Union Army to gather as much information as possible. Unfortunately, he was delayed on several occasions by unfortunate circumstances and did not report back to General Lee until July 2, thus depriving Lee of his eyes and ears at this most crucial point in the campaign. Lee now had no idea where the Union Army might be, or just how strong they were. Indeed, on June 28, he was alarmed to learn that the Union Army was massed in the vicinity of Frederick, Maryland, just thirty miles south of Gettysburg.

**Day One:** At 5 A.M. on July 1 the two armies finally blundered into each other about two miles west of Gettysburg when General Henry Heth's brigade discovered Union cavalry soldiers under General John Buford firmly entrenched atop Seminary Ridge, an elevation west of town. And now the first shots of the great battle rang out. Heth pushed ahead with two brigades of infantry against the Federals, but an hour into the battle, Union general John F. Reynolds arrived on the scene and committed the First and Eleventh Corps to the fight. Several hours later Heth's heavily outnumbered men were forced to withdraw, losing several hundred prisoners and the opportunity to take Gettysburg cheaply.

That afternoon, having learned of the battle, General Ewell dispatched Jubal Early and Robert Rodes to join the fight. At that point, General Lee arrived and ordered Heth's division to come to Rodes' support. An hour later Jubal Early's men arrived and attacked from the north, badly defeating the Union Eleventh Corps. Later that afternoon D. H. Hill's men finally cleared the First Corps from their positions atop Seminary Ridge. The First Corps then fled in disorder through the city to Cemetery Ridge, a mile and a half south of Gettysburg. Confederate soldiers under D. H. Hill and Richard Ewell were too exhausted to continue the attack, and thus the first day of fighting came to a close. At this point, the North has suffered some 9,000 casualties, the South 6,800.

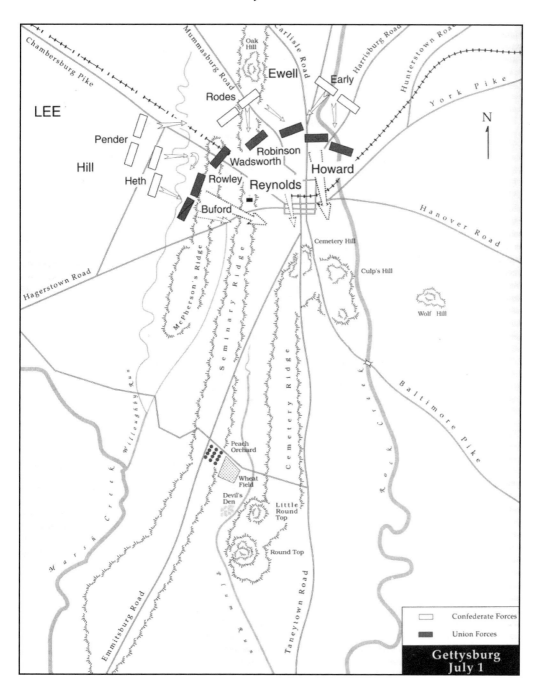

Gettysburg, Pennsylvania, July 1, 1863.

The South had clearly won the first day's battle, though the Union had won a strategic victory. For despite their retreat through the city, the Federals had managed to select their defensive positions, while Lee, without the services of Jeb Stuart, was placed in the position of having to attack over unfamiliar land. Still, Lee was determined to exploit his victory of Day One by renewing the fight on July 2.

**Day Two:** Early in the morning of July 2 Lee discovered that the Federals had occupied a horseshoe-shaped position, running from Culp's Hill to Cemetery Ridge and then down Cemetery Ridge. Lee ordered James Longstreet to take John Bell Hood's and Lafayette McLaws' divisions, a total of some 20,000 men, and strike the Federals' left flank. Their attack would be covered by D. H. Hill's corps. Richard Ewell, meanwhile, was to threaten Culp's Hill and Cemetery Hill (the Union right flank and center) in order to keep those Federals in place. Longstreet was strongly opposed to this plan and suggested that Lee should take a position from which the Confederates could fight a defensive battle. But Lee refused to listen, and thus the attack was set in motion over Longstreet's objections. Lee, unfortunately, was unaware that the entire Army of the Potomac was now in position just to his front.

Not until 3 P.M. did Longstreet's artillery attack get underway. Thirty minutes later his infantry began to move forward. Devil's Den and Little Round Top were struck first. For a long while the battle ebbed and flowed around Little Round Top, but Federal reinforcements finally arrived and forced Longstreet's withdrawal.

From the Devil's Den the battle spread north to the Wheatfield and then to the Peach Orchard. Within two hours the heavily outnumbered Confederates had carried the day and the Federal defenses had collapsed.

On Lee's left flank Richard Ewell ordered his artillery to open up at the moment he heard Longstreet's guns. Two hours later he sent his infantry forward. General Edward Johnson's division attacked Culp's Hill, while Jubal Early's division stormed Cemetery Hill. Johnson's men found the going tough against the entrenched Federals on Culp's Hill, though Early's men did manage to rout several regiments of Union infantry and capture several artillery pieces on Cemetery Hill. But then a Federal counterattack drove them back.

Day Two of the fight is considered a stalemate. The Confederates were still on the attack, though Union forces still held their positions.

**Day Three:** As Day Two came to a close, Lee had a decision to make. He could withdraw his army to the safety of Virginia, or he could assume a defensive position and wait for Meade to attack, as Longstreet had urged him to do, or he could continue his assault on the Federal lines. With unlimited confidence in his southern troops, he finally determined to continue his attack on July 3.

Longstreet, now reinforced by General George Pickett's division, was to renew his attack at dawn. Johnson's division, now reinforced, was to attack Culp's Hill at the same time. Stuart's cavalry, having finally found Lee's army, was to ride around the Union left flank and threaten them from the rear.

Unfortunately for the South, General Meade counterattacked at Culp's Hill an hour before dawn, thus disrupting Lee's strategy for today's battle. Lee then decided to launch a massive frontal attack in order to break the Union's center on Cemetery Ridge. A bombardment from 140 guns would cripple Union defenders prior to the

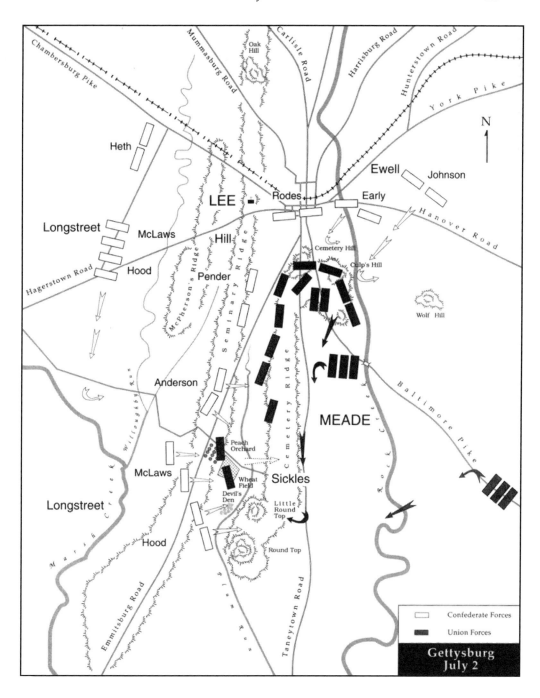

Gettysburg, Pennsylvania, July 2, 1863.

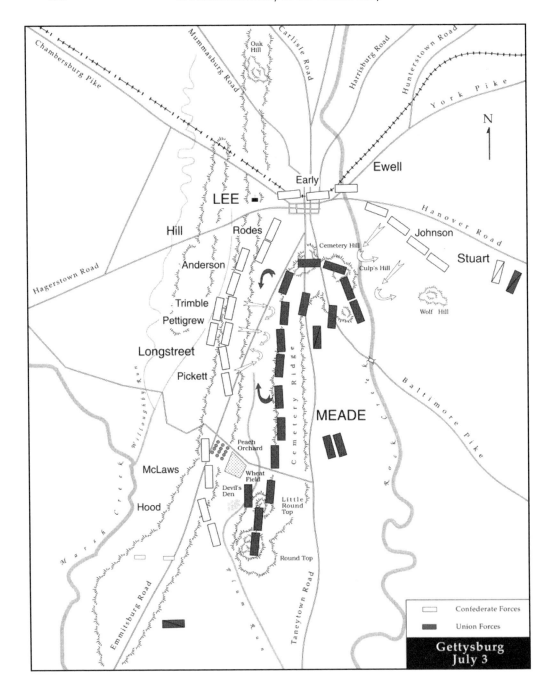

Gettysburg, Pennsylvania, July 3, 1863.

attack, and then the divisions of George Pickett, James Johnston Pettigrew and Isaac Trimble would advance over a mile of open ground to smash the Federal defenses.

It was a daring plan, and Longstreet, who was responsible for directing the attack, was adamantly opposed to it. In the end, however, Lee brushed aside Longstreet's objections and the attack commenced.

At 1:00 P.M. the cannon fire began. Over a hundred Union cannons responded, and thus ensued the largest cannon fight of the war. Two hours later southern guns had exhausted their ammunition and were unable to support the infantry once the attack began.

It was then that Longstreet very reluctantly ordered the advance, and Confederate infantry, 15,000 of the South's best and bravest, a perfect line of men that extended for over a mile, began their long march across a mile of open fields. Federal artillery opened fire at that point and inflicted terrible damage among those heroic southerners. But still they came. Finally, they broke into a run, and as they drew nearer, Union infantry added small-arms fire to the canister of the cannons, and the Confederates began to fall by the thousands. Finally, with the field now littered with southern dead, a small group of survivors led by General Lewis Armistead managed to leap over the low stone wall atop Cemetery Ridge and penetrate the Federal position, but Armistead was killed and his soldiers were quickly overwhelmed.

By 4:00 P.M. the attack had ended, and the South had suffered tragic losses. It was later estimated that as many as 6,000 men went down in a futile effort to break the Union center on Cemetery Ridge. And all for nothing.

The following day Lee waited and hoped for a Federal attack on his lines, but such an attack never came, and thus the Confederate Army began the long retreat to Virginia under a heavy rain that prevented Union pursuit. They crossed the Potomac on the evening of July 13.

This excursion northward had cost the South some 22,000 casualties, men that could not be replaced at this point in the war. It might be noted that Lee began his retreat on the same day that General Pemberton was surrendering Vicksburg to the Union.

**Bristoe Station, Virginia, October 14, 1863:** Located eight miles south of Manassas, this was the site of General A. P. Hill's most stunning defeat of the entire war. Earlier General Lee had received word that General Meade has transferred two corps from his army to Tennessee, and thus he decided to exploit this weakness by again taking the offensive. By attacking Bristoe Station, he hoped to draw Meade away from the railway junction at Culpeper and sever the Federals' line of communication with Washington.

On October 14, Hill's corps occupied the high ground at Bristoe Station. Below them the Federal army was caught up in a horrendous traffic jam of men, horses and wagons trying to ford the swollen Broad Run. Hill thus immediately ordered an attack on what appeared to be a disorganized Federal force.

But Hill, new at commanding a corps, made two major mistakes. First, he failed to scout the area with proper care. And, second, he sent only two brigades to attack a Federal force several times larger.

By the time the attack commenced Hill discovered to his horror that still another

Federal corps, one that Hill had not been aware of, was stationed squarely on the right flank of the attacking Southerners. This became one of the deadliest traps of the entire war.

The fighting that afternoon lasted for only forty minutes as Hill's southern soldiers were cut to pieces. The Twenty-Seventh North Carolina lost over half its men, including 33 of 36 officers. In all, Hill suffered 1,400 casualties in this battle, the Union fewer than 600. (See battle map.)

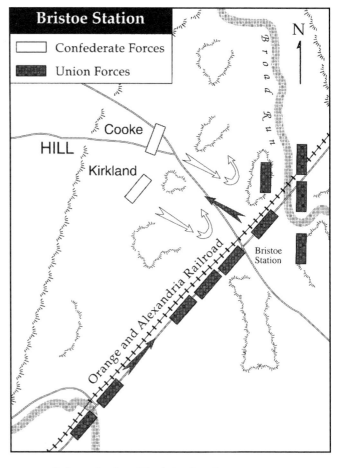

Bristoe Station, Virginia, October 14, 1863.

## 1863 — South and West

**Vicksburg, Missis-sippi, April–July, 1863:** By the first of the year General Grant had determined to open the Mississippi River and divide the South. The key to this operation, obviously, was the heavily fortified city of Vicksburg. This time Grant would land his force in Louisiana, on the west side of the Mississippi, then have them transported by boat into the state of Mississippi, and attack Vicksburg from the east. This he did, and on May 7 his army of 44,000 men defeated a force of 6,000 Confederates at Jackson. He then turned west in order to attack Vicksburg from the rear. At Champion's Hill they met and defeated a force under General John C. Pemberton. The following day, at Big Black River, Pemberton's badly outnumbered Confederates were again defeated, and forced to withdraw to Vicksburg. On May 19 Grant ordered an all-out assault on Confederate positions in that city, but his men were defeated all along the line. Three days later the Confederates again turned away a heavy assault. Thus Grant saw that he would be forced to undertake a siege, which he had hoped to avoid.

By early July, after a 47-day siege, dozens of Confederate soldiers and citizens were daily dying of starvation. Thus General Pemberton had no choice but to surrender the beleaguered city. Grant, in turn, offered to parole Pemberton's army, allow

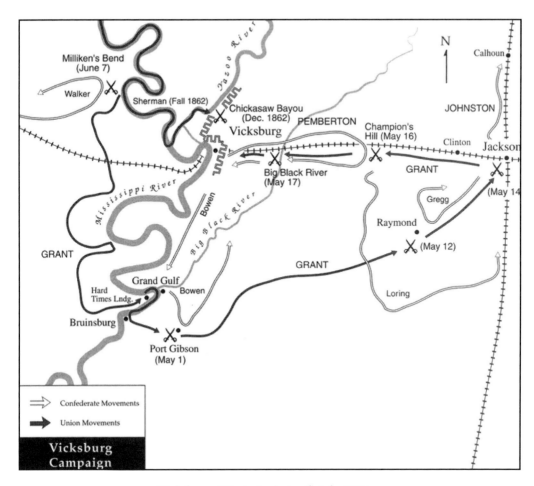

Vicksburg, Mississippi, April–July, 1863.

officers to keep their sidearms and one horse each. And thus on July 4, 1863, Vicksburg was surrendered, and now the Union controlled the entire Mississippi River. It was a terrible blow to the South. (See battle map.)

**Morris Island, South Carolina, July–September, 1863:** Earlier, the Confederacy had erected two forts, Fort Wagner and Battery Gregg, as the principal land defenses of Morris Island, which commanded the only approach to Charleston Harbor. Fort Wagner was an enclosed earthwork that extended across a narrow point of the island and was designed to prevent an enemy attack on Battery Gregg by land. Between July 10 and July 18 a few Confederate troops turned back repeated assaults from a vastly superior Union force, thus delaying for months the Union's plan to capture Charleston.

The Union force was composed of a combination army-navy contingent commanded by General Quincy Gillmore and Admiral John Dahlgren. Their major goal was to seize Morris Island from which they could reduce the defenses of Charleston and thus capture that city. On July 10 Union general George Strong landed his brigade of 3,700 troops on the island despite spirited resistance from the Confederates in Wagner and Gregg. Strong lost 106 men in that landing, the South 294.

The following day, July 11, unaware that Wagner had been reinforced during the previous night, bringing its number of defenders up to some 1,200 men under the command of General William Booth Taliaferro, Strong ordered three of his regiments forward in a daylight assault on Fort Wagner. By day's end the Confederates had repeatedly beaten back charge after charge from Strong's Federals, costing them some 350 casualties. The South lost six men killed, six wounded.

Following this fiasco, there was a three-day lull in the fighting while the Union brought ashore heavy siege artillery. To cover the placement of these pieces, Union naval vessels subjected Wagner to a constant bombardment, shelling the well-dug-in Confederates without pause for three days and nights—but with little effect. Indeed, southern losses were recorded as eight killed, twenty wounded.

At that time, in addition to its 1,200 troops, Wagner was armed with 13 heavy guns and one light field piece, hardly a match for the tremendous firepower employed by Union forces.

After three days of shelling, a second assault on the fort was ordered for the evening of July 18.

At dusk on that evening, Federal infantry, consisting of Strong's and Colonel Henry Putnam's brigades, supported by General Thomas Stevenson's brigade — a force of over 6,000 men — began their advance on the fort.

Leading this attack was the Fifty-fourth Massachusetts Regiment, a much-celebrated black regiment under the command of Colonel Robert G. Shaw.

By midnight, after hours of bloody hand-to-hand fighting, the Federals finally gained a foothold in the fort. But then Taliaferro's small but determined Confederate force rallied and drove the Federals out. Indeed, the Union retreat became a rout as blue-clad soldiers fled back to their lines in panic. Their losses in this night's fighting were heavy, with 246 killed, 880 wounded, and 389 missing. Among the dead were General Strong, Colonel Putnam and five regimental commanders. The Confederates, on the other hand, suffered 36 killed, 133 wounded and five missing.

At this point General Gillmore abandoned his efforts to capture Morris Island by direct assaults and settled back for a long siege operation. Some seven weeks later, on September 6, having depleted their stores of food and water, the Confederates were forced to abandon the island under the cover of darkness. The Union Army quickly occupied the island, and from there they mercilessly rained shot and shell down on the women and children of Charleston.

**The Bombardment of Charleston, August 22, 1863 — War's End:** Early in the war the Federal military saw the importance of capturing Charleston. Not only was it the hated birthplace of secession, but it was also a center for southern arms manufacturing and a port for blockade runners. They tried twice, in June of '62 and April of '63, but neither attempt was successful. Thus came their attempts to capture Morris Island, which also proved unsuccessful.

Still, General Gillmore did occupy much of Morris Island, and from there he trained his rifled long-range guns on Charleston, some four miles away. On August 21 he sent a message to General P. G. T. Beauregard, the commanding officer of

Charleston, demanding the immediate surrender of the city or shelling would commence within four hours. Beauregard dashed off a reply charging that by not giving "timely notice" to the citizens of Charleston Gillmore was committing "an act of barbarity." Still, in the early morning hours of August 22, 1863, the bombardment of Charleston began.

Citizens of Charleston who could afford to leave did so, taking carriages, wagons and trains to safer communities. Banks, hospitals and offices were moved north of Calhoun Street, beyond the range of Gillmore's big guns. The city's orphanage was moved to Orangeburg.

Following the opening of the bombardment, blockade running came to a virtual standstill. The cost of goods and services skyrocketed, and destitution was widespread. Public schools were closed and, since most of the city's firemen were now in the army, fires raced unchecked through the downtown area.

In mid–April of 1864 General Beauregard was ordered to North Carolina, and in his place as commander of southern forces in

The Bombardment of Charleston

Bombardment of Charleston, August 22, 1863–February 18, 1865.

Charleston came General Samuel Jones. By this time the Union Army held all of Morris Island and its artillery was pounding Fort Sumter into rubble.

In October of '64 General William Hardee replaced General Jones in Charleston to take command of the 12,000 troops located in that general area. In late November Hardee turned over the defense of Charleston to General Robert Ransom and headed south for Savannah, taking several thousand troops with him to meet General Sherman's army of 60,000 battle-hardened soldiers.

A month later Hardee retreated to Charleston with 16,000 troops, but by mid–February he saw that defending the city was no longer possible and thus he and his troops began a long northward trek to join General Joe Johnston's army in North Carolina.

On February 18, 1865, Charleston was finally surrendered to Union forces. By this time the siege had lasted for 587 days. (See battle map.)

**Chickamauga Creek, Tennessee, September 19–20, 1863:** Following Confederate defeats at Gettysburg, Vicksburg and Knoxville, the South experienced a decisive victory at Chickamauga, one that was badly needed, one that brought new life to the cause. It might be pointed out that this was one of the few battles during the war where southern troops (66,000) outnumbered Union troops (58,000).

The battle at Chickamauga actually began in the early summer of '63 when General Rosecrans' Army of the Cumberland moved from Murfreesboro towards General Braxton Bragg's Army of Tennessee positioned around Chattanooga. Fearing that he was badly outnumbered, on September 9 Bragg abandoned Chattanooga and retreated south in hopes of preventing Rosecrans from invading north Georgia.

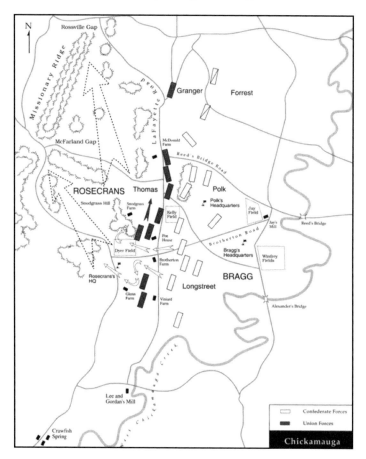

On September 19, however, his troops now reinforced, Bragg moved to position his army between Chattanooga and Rosecrans' widely separated corps. He chose Chickamauga Creek, about ten miles south of Chattanooga, which he would use to anchor his left flank, near Lee and Gordon's Mill.

On September 19 the two armies clashed in the heavily wooded hills around Chickamauga Creek. By nightfall neither side seemed to have gained an advantage. It was then, however, that General Longstreet arrived with heavy reinforcements from the Army of Northern Virginia. The following morning the Confederates again

Chickamauga Creek, Tennessee, September 19–29, 1863.

attacked, driving back Union forces, except for their left flank commanded by General George H. Thomas. That afternoon, Rosecrans, believing that his troops had been badly defeated, ordered a general retreat to Chattanooga. Bragg, unaware that he had won a major victory, failed to pursue the fleeing Union Army, and thus lost an excellent chance to destroy the Army of the Cumberland.

The South suffered some 18,000 casualties in this battle, the North 16,000.

A month following this northern debacle, General Grant replaced Rosecrans as commander of the Army of the Cumberland. (See battle map.)

**Lookout Mountain and Missionary Ridge, Tennessee, November 24, 1863:** Located a few miles south of Chattanooga and the Tennessee River, Lookout Mountain, which Bragg considered an impregnable position, was occupied by several thousand Confederate troops, with the majority of the army strung along the sharp, steep bluffs of Missionary Ridge, which extended for several miles southeast of Chattanooga. On November 24 General Hooker's men attacked Lookout Mountain and, to everyone's surprise, drove the Confederates from their positions. The following day Grant's troops formed in the valley below Missionary Ridge. Within a few minutes the Union men had routed the southerners. Indeed, generals Bragg and Breckinridge barely escaped capture. To this day no one has been able to offer an explanation for the complete collapse of the Confederates in this engagement.

A week following this southern debacle, Jefferson Davis replaced Braxton Bragg, one of his dearest friends, as commander of the Army of Tennessee with Joseph Johnston, whom Davis thoroughly disliked.

## 1864 — Northern Virginia

**The Wilderness, May 5–6, 1864:** On the evening of May 4 General Meade's Army of the Potomac (General Ulysses S. Grant accompanied Meade on this foray and was actually giving the commands), a huge force of some 120,000 men, camped at the edge of the Wilderness, a wild expanse of forest not far from Fredericksburg and Chancellorsville. His plan was to move past Lee's right flank before Lee could react, and position his army between Lee and Richmond. Unfortunately for Grant, he awakened the next morning to find his army confronted by Robert E. Lee's Army of Northern Virginia, a force of some 65,000 men. There were two major roads through the Wilderness, roads that Grant would have to use in his march to Richmond. One, the Orange Turnpike, was now occupied by Richard Ewell's Second Corps. The other, the Orange Plank Road, two miles north, was occupied by A. P. Hill's Third Corps. James Longstreet's First Corps was miles away and would not reach the battle until the following day.

Throughout that first day the two armies struggled, the heavy undergrowth making cavalry or artillery operations nearly impossible. The southerners were suffering terrible casualties, men who could not be replaced, while those who did survive were too exhausted to go on.

On the morning of May 6 a massive Union assault rolled over Hill's tattered remnants and threatened to destroy the entire southern army. It was at this crucial point that Longstreet's First Corps arrived. And it was then that General Lee himself seized command of the veteran Texas Brigade and led it into the teeth of the Union Army. (The Texas Brigade would suffer 50 percent casualties in this encounter.)

Unbelievably, four brigades of Longstreet's corps, under the command of General Micah Jenkins, managed to slip past Grant's left flank, then mount a charge which totally routed the Union line. (During the fighting friendly fire killed General Jenkins and severely wounded Longstreet.) Later in the evening General John B. Gordon's men destroyed the Union right flank, capturing two Union generals in the process. Indeed, Lee and his southerners had achieved an amazing victory against a vastly superior force on day two of the fighting.

Throughout the next day the two armies merely held their ground, with neither

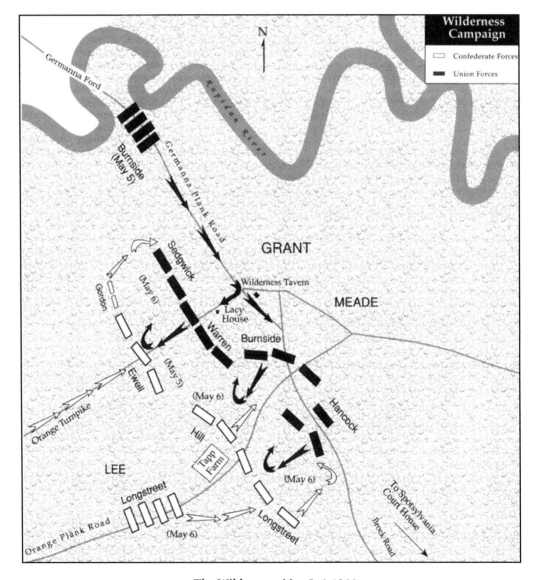

The Wilderness, May 5–6, 1864.

willing to renew the fighting. As soon as feasible, Grant withdrew his beaten army and began a race for Spotsylvania Court House. The Federals suffered 18,000 casualties in this campaign, the South 8,000. (See battle map.)

**Spotsylvania Court House, Virginia, May 8–12, 1864:** Following the two-day fight at the Wilderness, Grant ordered Meade to move his army twelve miles to the southeast to Spotsylvania Court House. That evening, under cover of darkness, Lee also decided to move his First Corps to the same location. These forces collided on the morning of the eighth, and throughout the day they were reinforced by additional units.

Lee, of course, was at a disadvantage since General Longstreet was out of action with a wound received two days earlier, and General A. P. Hill was too ill to mount his horse. General Richard Anderson was thus placed in command of the First Corps, while Jubal Early assumed command of Hill's Third Corps.

On May 9 General Burnside assumed a position east of the village. Lee immediately dispatched Early to oppose the Federals there. (It was here that a southern sharpshooter killed General John Sedgwick.) Later that morning General Philip Sheridan led his cavalry corps southward on a raid towards Richmond. Lee immediately dispatched Jeb Stuart's cavalry and General Fitzhugh Lee's division to pursue them. Two days later Stuart was wounded in an engagement at Yellow Tavern, and would die the next day in Richmond. This was another terrible blow for the South.

The terrible fighting at Spotsylvania would reach a climax on May 12 as the two armies engaged in a savage struggle for a strategic position to the front of Ewell's

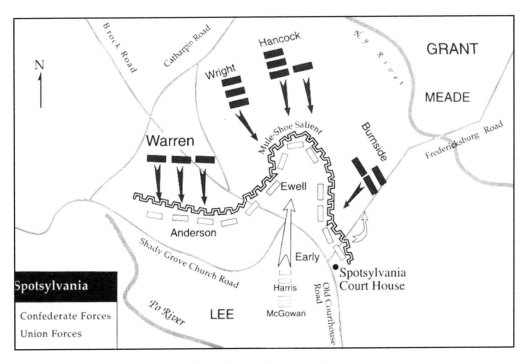

Spotsylvania Court House, Virginia, May 8–12, 1864.

Third Corps, very aptly called the Bloody Angle. Of this fight, one Union officer wrote: "It was chiefly a hand to hand fight across the breastworks. Rank after rank was riddled by shot and shell and bayonet thrusts, and finally sank, a mass of mutilated corpses; then fresh troops rushed madly forward to replace the dead, and so the murderous work went on. Guns were run up close to the parapet, and double charges of canister played their part in the bloody work. The fence rails and logs in the breastworks were shattered into splinters, and trees over a foot and a half in diameter were cut completely in two by the incessant musketry fire."

Indeed, the fight at Bloody Angle has been called the most intense period of land warfare up to that time. Both armies, having suffered heavy casualties, departed Spotsylvania Court House on May 22. The Union, with unlimited supplies of men and materials, could replace its losses. The South could not. (See battle map.)

**Yellow Tavern, Virginia, May 11, 1864:** As the fighting raged at the Wilderness and Spotsylvania, General Meade dispatched General Philip Sheridan and his seven cavalry brigades, a force of some 10,000 men, towards Richmond with orders to isolate and destroy Jeb Stuart's cavalry. When informed of this strategy, Stuart immediately mobilized his three cavalry brigades, some 4,000 men, and went in pursuit of Sheridan. He arrived at Yellow Tavern two days later, on May 11, and lay in wait for the Federals. At eleven that morning Sheridan began positioning his troops in front of Stuart's lines. For the next three hours the southerners beat back wave after wave of Union attacks. Then at four that afternoon, General George Armstrong Custer launched a gigantic attack against Stuart's center and left flank, commanded by General Lunsford Lindsay Lomax. At that point Stuart rode to the left to lend encouragement to Lomax's men. Then came another wave of Federals. In the ensuing battle the Confederates rallied and pushed Custer's men back behind the Union lines. It was at this point that a retreating Federal soldier shot Stuart in his right side. The ball pierced his abdomen and lodged in his body. That evening, after a long and bloody struggle, as his heavily outnumbered men finally turned Sheridan's cavalry back from Richmond, Stuart was taken by ambulance to his brother-in-law's home in Richmond. He died the next day. As a result of this battle, Sheridan abandoned his drive for Richmond and moved his cavalry thirty miles southeast down the Chickahominy River.

**New Market, Virginia, May 15, 1864:** In hopes of wresting control of the Shenandoah Valley from the Confederates, a Union force of 9,000 soldiers under General Franz Sigel invaded the valley in early May. Opposing him were 4,100 southerners (including 250 members of the Corps of Cadets from Virginia Military Institute) under General John C. Breckinridge. These two forces collided on the morning of May 15. Breckinridge immediately seized the offensive and charged Sigel's army, causing the Federals to withdraw. New Market has been called the "biggest little battle of the war" since it allowed the South to control the Shenandoah throughout the summer of '64.

**Drewry's Bluff, Virginia, May 16, 1864:** Located only seven miles from Richmond, Drewry's Bluff became the scene of a great battle following the Union's landing of Gen. Ben Butler's 39,000 troops at Bermuda Hundred earlier in the month, making both Richmond and Petersburg vulnerable to attack.

Butler's position was too strong to be successfully attacked by frontal assault, thus General P. G. T. Beauregard sent General Robert F. Hoke to Drewery's Bluff in hopes that his force of 20,000 Confederates could draw Butler's men out into the open. On May 12 Butler, leaving half his troops behind, took the bait and advanced 25,000 troops to Drewery's Bluff. They attacked the following day with some success, but Butler failed to follow up on his success and called a halt to the Federal advance.

By the following day Beauregard himself arrived on the scene. He immediately ordered Confederates under General Robert Ransom to attack Butler's right flank at dawn on May 16. This they did and with great initial success. But a early morning fog set in and the attack became disjointed. By late afternoon Butler's force began their retreat to Bermuda Hundred. This fight cost the Union 4,160 casualties, the South 2,506. But it had ended Butler's threat to Richmond and Petersburg.

**Cold Harbor, Virginia, May 31, 1864:** In his drive to capture Richmond and destroy the Army of Northern Virginia in the bargain, Grant next moved his Army of the Potomac southeast across the Pamunkey River to Cold Harbor. By June 1 Lee began feeding troops into that area. Both armies began to dig entrenchments, so that soon there were two six-mile-long fortifications running northwest to southeast.

On the morning of June 3 Grant attacked Lee's right flank under General A. P. Hill and the center under General Richard Anderson. But the southerners put up a withering fire. Indeed, Union soldiers fell in such numbers that the battle was over in fifteen minutes. Grant and his generals then cancelled plans for further attacks. The Union lost 12,000 men in this engagement, the South 1,500.

As a result, Grant abandoned his plans to

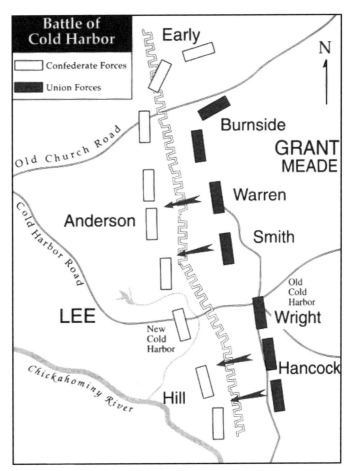

Cold Harbor, Virginia, May 31, 1864.

engage Lee's Army of Northern Virginia with frontal attacks. Instead, he would begin a siege of Petersburg. (See battle map.)

**Petersburg, Virginia, June 15, 1864–April 3, 1865:** In an effort to break the stalemate that existed at Cold Harbor, Grant moved his army to Petersburg. All the railroads that connected Richmond with its supply lines ran through Petersburg, and if that city fell the South would be forced to fight without supplies, an impossible situation. On June 15, General William Smith's 12,500 Union soldiers overwhelmed General Henry A. Wise's 2,200 Confederates and occupied over three miles of the line surrounding Petersburg. The following day General P. G. T. Beauregard arrived with a force of 14,000 to face a Union Army that now numbered approximately 80,000. That city might have fallen on July 17 after Confederate lines were twice shattered. But heroic counterattacks by General Bushrod Rust Johnson's heavily outnumbered division drove the invaders back. At this point, after three days of fighting, the North had already lost some 10,500 men, while the South had lost about 4,000.

With the arrival of Lee's forces in late June the South now had 50,000 men covering a line twenty-six miles long from Richmond to Petersburg. Grant, on the other hand, now had about 112,000 men to assault that line. But despite their superior numbers, nothing the Union tried could break the southern line.

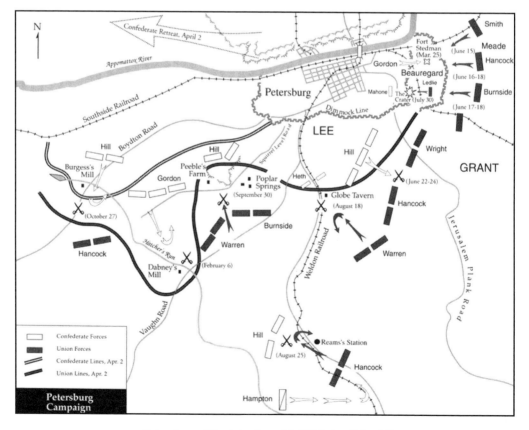

Petersburg, Virginia, June 15, 1864–April 3, 1865.

Thus in late July Grant decided to halt his ineffectual frontal attacks and use another, more radical, strategy. In hopes of avoiding a long siege, such as he had used at Vicksburg, Grant had coal miners from the Forty-eighth Pennsylvania dig a tunnel 511 feet long to the Confederate line (directly under General Stephen Elliot's salient), and then they packed it with eight thousand pounds of black powder. Grant then chose General James Ledlie's division to spearhead the attack once the explosion took place.

At 4:40 A.M. an incredible explosion blasted a hole 170 feet long, 60 feet wide, and 30 feet deep in the Confederate line. Then 15,000 Federal troops from the Ninth Corps rushed into the crater. But their commander, General Ledlie, was back behind Union lines hiding in a dugout, and thus the men had no leadership. They simply milled about, laughing and talking, and picking up and examining personal items which they stumbled across in the debris.

Within minutes the southerners recovered from their initial shock and a division led by General William Mahone counterattacked and slaughtered hundreds of Federals caught in the crater and drove back the others to their own lines. By 1:00 P.M. the battle was over. Grant's latest fiasco had cost his army 4,000 men and led to a congressional investigation.

Grant now knew that only a long siege would reduce Petersburg and open the way to Richmond. (See battle map.)

**Monocacy River, Virginia (Jubal Early's Washington Raid), July 9, 1864:** In hopes of forcing General Grant to reduce the number of troops facing him at Petersburg, General Lee ordered General Jubal Early to take his corps up the Shenandoah Valley to threaten Washington. On July 9 at a point on the Monocacy River only thirty miles from the Capital, Early was confronted by a small force of Federal troops. Unfortunately, Early was delayed long enough for Grant to send heavy reinforcements, and he was forced to retreat. (See battle map.)

**Winchester, Fisher's Hill, and Cedar Creek, Virginia, September 19–22, 1864:** In early September General Grant sent General Philip Sheridan and his cavalry, a force of some 50,000 men, to the Shenandoah Valley with orders to devastate that fertile area in order to deprive General Lee of his main source of

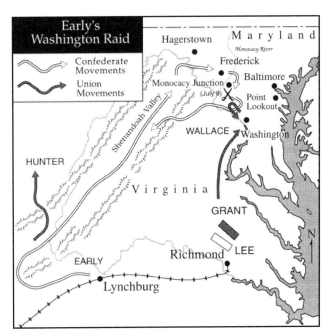

Monocacy River, Virginia (Jubal Early's Washington Raid), July 9, 1864.

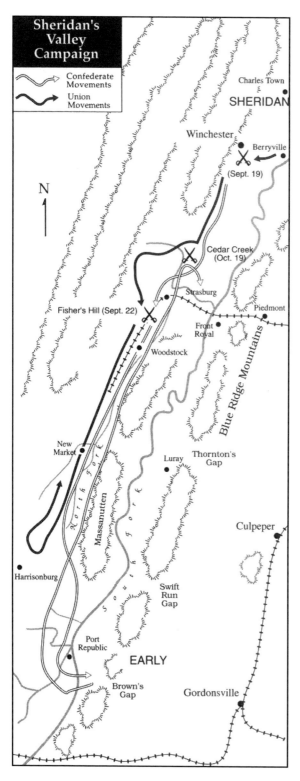

food and forage. For several weeks Sheridan went about his work with relish, opposed only by southern women and children. But then General Lee dispatched Jubal Early with a force of 25,000 to put an end to Sheridan's work. Unfortunately, Early was defeated at Winchester, and three days later he was defeated at Fisher's Hill. Early then received reinforcements and reformed his army. On October 19 he attacked Sheridan at Cedar Creek. Initially, the Confederates were successful, sending the Federals reeling back in confusion. But then came a counterattack which carried the day for the Union, and with evening Early retreated. From this point on, the Shenandoah would be of no value to the Confederacy. (See battle map.)

## 1864 — South and West

**Meridian, Mississippi, February 3–14, 1864:** In the winter of 1863-64, General Sherman decided to remove all Confederate threats to the Mississippi River, especially those areas east of the river. Of special interest to Sherman was Meridian, Mississippi, a railway center critical to southern communications and supply. Another goal, said Sherman, was "to punish the rebel General Nathan Bedford Forrest."

Sherman's plan was to send 17,000 troops from Memphis by steamboat, and gather another 10,000 from Vicksburg, a total of almost 30,000 soldiers.

Opposing Sherman was General

**Winchester, Fisher's Hill, and Cedar Creek, Virginia, September 19–22, 1864.**

Leonidas Polk, who was headquartered at Meridian. He had only 9,000 men, plus General Stephen D. Lee's cavalry corps of 7,500 men. Also, Nathan Bedford Forrest and his cavalry of 3,000 was riding hard to reach Meridian before Sherman could arrive.

To confuse the southerners, Sherman dispatched several companies by steamer to feint an attack on Yazoo City. But those soldiers disembarked to find themselves face to face with General Lawrence Ross' Texas Brigade. The Texans, armed with pistols, charged the attacking Federals at the edge of the river and began firing at point-blank range. Those Federals who managed to survive fled back to their steamboats and escaped up river.

On February 7, Sherman camped at Decatur, a village about twenty miles west of Meridian. During the night Confederate Colonel Wirt Adams' cavalry attacked the sleeping Federals, and Sherman himself narrowly escaped capture before the southerners retreated.

On the evening of February 14 Sherman's army finally reached Meridian only to find that General Polk's men had fled. There they began a systematic campaign of destruction. Whatever they could not steal, they burned. And they destroyed miles of railroad track.

With this accomplished, Sherman's other goal, to destroy Forrest, remained. But in this, according to Sherman, "we failed utterly."

Indeed, Union General William Smith's 7,000 cavalrymen encountered Forrest near West Point and fought for some two hours before the Federals retreated, Forrest's men in pursuit. For almost eighty miles the Federals retreated back towards Memphis with Forrest on their tail. By the next day Smith had suffered 388 casualties, Forrest 144.

By February 20 Sherman had grown tired of waiting for Smith and began moving back to Vicksburg. But here he perfected the type of warfare for which he would later become infamous. This campaign had cost him only 500 casualties; Southern casualties are not known.

**Fort Pillow, Tennessee, April 12, 1864:** Located on the Mississippi River forty miles north of Memphis, Fort Pillow had been occupied by Federal troops since the early summer of 1862. In April of '64 its garrison consisted of one regiment of Union Tennessee troops and four companies of

Meridian, Mississippi, February 3–14, 1864.

African-American artillery, some 557 men in all. On April 12 Nathan Bedford Forrest and his 1,500 cavalrymen positioned themselves around the fort. Then, under a flag of truce, Forrest informed the Union commander that the fort was surrounded, and demanded an immediate surrender. When the commander refused, Forrest ordered an attack. After a short fight, the garrison fled towards the river with Forrest's men in pursuit, killing many along the way. Indeed, it was during the retreat that the Union suffered the majority of its fatalities, a total of some 221 men. Forrest was later accused of massacring helpless prisoners, a charge which he vociferously denied. Lending credence to his denials, it was pointed out that 336 Union soldiers survived this battle, 226 of them unhurt in any way.

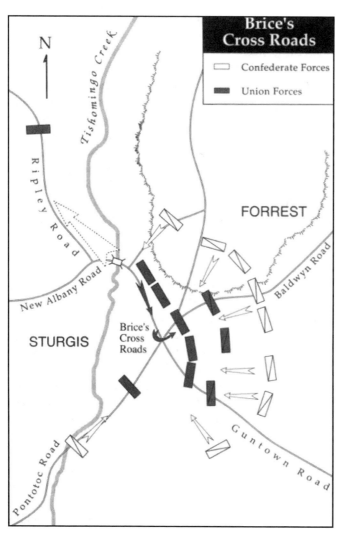

Brice's Cross Roads (Tishomingo Creek), Mississippi, June 10, 1864.

**Resaca, Georgia, May 13–14, 1864:** General Sherman now had under his command the Army of the Cumberland, the Army of the Tennessee, and the Army of the Ohio, some 98,000 men. He departed Chattanooga knowing that between him and Atlanta stood the Confederate Army of Tennessee, a force of some 45,000 men, under General Joseph Johnston located at Dalton. Johnston had divided his army into two corps, commanded by William J. Hardee and John Bell Hood. Also, Leonidas Polk, now located in Alabama, commanded a force of 14,000 troops that could be called on in an emergency. Thus Sherman decided to slip around Johnston to Resaca, some fifteen miles south of Dalton, a village defended by General James Cantey with about 1,400 men. On May 12 Johnston pulled his main army back to reinforce Cantey, thus delaying a Union attack. The real battle began on the afternoon of May 13 and lasted until nightfall. The fight recommenced the next morning and by evening the divisions of General Alexander Stewart and Carter Stevenson had driven the Federals back several miles. The next day the corps of Leonidas Polk arrived, giving Johnston some 60,000 men. Still, at that point, in order to protect his line of communication, Johnston evacuated Resaca. Thus Johnston began his retreat southward, fighting as he went, his object to make Sherman's advance as slow and costly as possible. The Confederates suffered some 5,000 casualties at Resaca, the Federals about 6,500.

**Brice's Cross Roads (Tishomingo Creek), Mississippi, June 10, 1864:** In an effort to prevent General Nathan Bedford Forrest from destroying his supply lines, General Sherman dispatched General Samuel D. Sturgis and his cavalry to corner and destroy Forrest. In early June Sturgis started out with a force of 9,000 men, three times the size of Forrest's cavalry. On June 10 they collided at Brice's Cross Roads in northern Mississippi. From the very beginning, Sturgis' campaign became a comedy of errors, with his horsemen entangled with their supply train, guns mired in the mud, and his supporting infantry too exhausted to be of any help. On the night of the tenth, Sturgis himself was nowhere to be found, so his senior officers decided to retreat. Forced to leave behind their sick and wounded, their retreat was hampered by Forrest's wild horsemen. Sturgis had lost over 2,500 men, and Forrest was still free to conduct his hit-and-run attacks just as he had always done. (See battle map.)

**Kenesaw Mountain, Georgia, June 27, 1864:** By June 27 Sherman had lost his patience. Repeatedly, he had flanked the wily Johnston only to see him retreat with few casualties to another and apparently stronger position. Now Johnston was firmly entrenched at Kenesaw Mountain, only twenty-five miles northwest of Atlanta. That day, the furious Sherman would not attempt to go around him but would attack from the front. He did, and lost 3,000 men in less than an hour. From now on a reformed Sherman would refuse to attack Johnston, but would return to his old flanking movements. Johnston requested that President Davis order Nathan Bedford Forrest's cavalry to destroy Sherman's supply lines in Tennessee, but Davis (aided and abetted by Braxton Bragg) was convinced that the commander of the Army of Tennessee needed more of a fighting spirit. Thus on July 17 Davis relieved the cautious Johnston of his command, replacing him with the impetuous John Bell Hood. (See battle map.)

**Peachtree Creek, July 20, 1864:** John Bell Hood did not have to be told that Davis expected him to take the offensive and wipe out Sherman's army as quickly as possible. On July 20 he attacked Union forces strung out along Peachtree Creek just north of Atlanta. After an all-day fight the corps of William Hardee and Alexander Stewart were repulsed with heavy losses. Two days later Hood again attacked, and again he was forced to withdraw with heavy losses.

**The Battle of Atlanta, July 22, 1864:** Hood now took up a strong position in Atlanta, still convinced that the best defense was a strong offense. Thus on July 22 he dispatched Hardee's corps to attack Union forces east of Atlanta. The South inflicted 4,000 casualties on Sherman in this battle, but suffered 7,500 casualties of its own. Some six weeks later Sherman had extended his lines until he threatened to

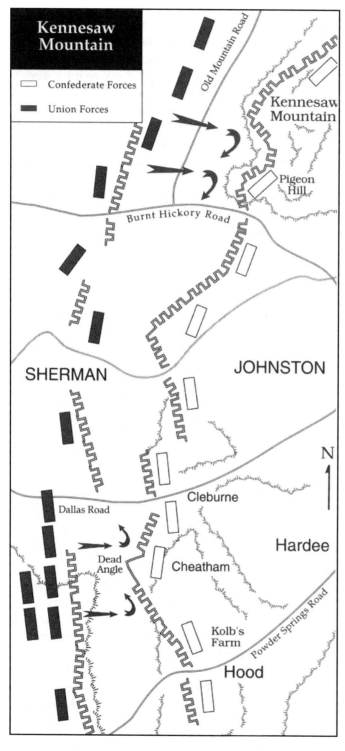

Kenesaw Mountain, Georgia, June 27, 1864.

capture the Montgomery and Atlanta Railroad, the one remaining railroad south of the city. Having lost 17,500 men in a series of engagements, Hood saw that his situation was critical. His last fight with Sherman took place at Jonesboro on August 31. He evacuated Atlanta on September 1, and Sherman took possession of the city the following day. (See battle map.)

**General Sterling Price's Missouri Raid, September–December, 1864:** While both Richmond and Atlanta were under siege, General Sterling Price, commander of the District of Arkansas and Missouri, and General Kirby Smith, commander of the Trans-Mississippi Department, laid plans to capture St. Louis which had been under Federal control since the fall of 1861. A victory here, reasoned Price, would re-capture Missouri for the Confederacy, claim thousands of recruits for his army, and encourage citizens in the North to vote Lincoln out of office in the upcoming presidential election.

On August 28 Price departed Camden, Arkansas, with three cavalry divisions under generals John Sappington Marmaduke

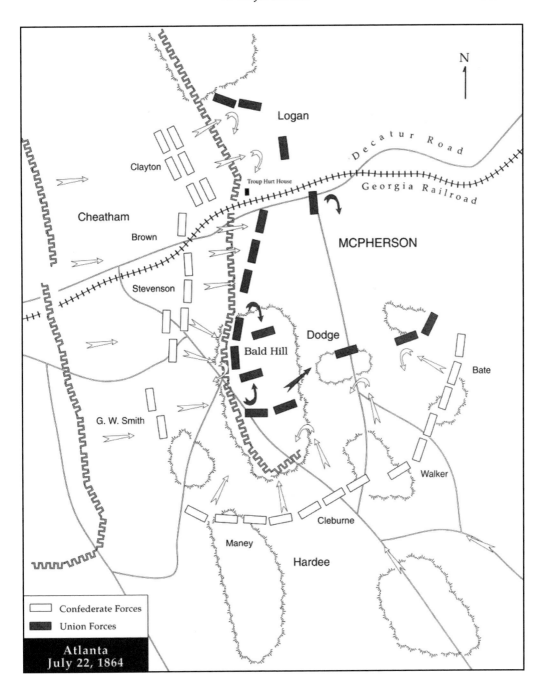

The Battle of Atlanta, July 22, 1864.

General Sterling Price's Missouri Raid, September–October, 1864.

and James Fagan, a force of 12,000 soldiers. After several brief skirmishes, Price attacked Federal troops at Fort Davidson, near Pilot Knob. But rather than bombarding Fort Davidson into submission, Price ordered a frontal assault across 900 yards of open meadow. Within twenty minutes his troops had suffered more than 1,000 casualties, the very best of his command. That night Price finally shelled the fort into submission. It was at this point that a dismayed Price was informed that Gen. A. J. Smith had reinforced the garrison at St. Louis with another 8,000 Union soldiers. Price realized that he could no longer capture that city.

Yet, he hoped he could still attract recruits and influence the outcome of the Federal election. Thus on September 30 he sent General Joseph O. Shelby's cavalry to threaten St. Louis while he led his main army westward along the Missouri River in the direction of Jefferson City. Four days later, having bypassed Jefferson City, he occupied Boonville, where he gathered 2,000 new recruits for his army. Then it was on to Glasgow where he captured 500 Union troops. By now, in addition to their 2,000 unarmed recruits, Price's invading army was burdened with 500 Union prisoners of war as well as 500 wagons loaded with captured Union supplies.

At this point, General William Rosecrans laid plans to destroy Price's army. Price became aware of Rosecrans' plans and that he would soon be surrounded by a force twice the size of his own. Thus he turned southward, and on October 21 he defeated a small force of 500 Federals at the Little Blue River. The following day Price's army defeated another Union force at the Big Blue River, but nightfall prevented a big southern victory. The following day, October 23, Price sent divisions under Shelby, Marmaduke and Fagan to attack the Federals at Westport. Briefly, it appeared that the Confederates would be successful here, but Marmaduke's men eventually ran out of ammunition and began a retreat that turned into a rout. Soon, a general retreat began all along the line as the Confederates fled for Santa Fe. Indeed, at this point, Price's retreat southward became a disorganized mass of horsemen, cattle, wagons and refugees. Two days later, at the Marais des Cygne River, Federals again attacked Price, but a stout defense allowed his army to escape across the river, though Marmaduke was captured in the fight. On October 28 Price marched his force across the Arkansas River and into Indian Territory. On November 23 they arrived at Bonham, Texas. By the time they had arrived back at Laynesport, Arkansas, on December 2, they had marched an incredible 1,488 miles and suffered over 4,000 casualties. (See battle map.)

**Franklin and Nashville, Tennessee, November 30–December 16, 1864:** In September of '64, while the army rested, President Davis and General Hood laid plans to pry Union forces out of Georgia, reasoning that an attack on the railroad connecting Union forces in Atlanta with their base at Chattanooga would compel them to withdraw northward in order to protect their supply line. Thus in October Hood moved into northwestern Georgia, striking against the railroad as he went. His army of 40,000 was divided into three corps, commanded by generals Alexander Stewart, Stephen D. Lee, and Benjamin Franklin Cheatham. Plus there was a cavalry corps under General Joseph Wheeler. They reached Gadsden, Alabama, on October 30.

But Sherman refused to be drawn from Atlanta. He dispatched part of his force to Tennessee, and with the rest he departed for Savannah.

Thus Hood hatched a new plan. He would turn northward towards Nashville. Hood made this move without consulting his commanding officer, General P. G. T. Beauregard. When informed of Hood's plan, Beauregard ordered him to dispatch Joseph Wheeler's cavalry to oppose Sherman's march to the sea, promising to send Nathan Bedford Forrest to replace Wheeler.

Not until November 20 did Hood get his entire force across the Tennessee River, and on the twenty-first they started for middle Tennessee. On the evening of November 28–29 Hood ordered the forces of Forrest, Cheatham, Stewart, and one division of Stephen D. Lee's corps to Spring Hill. The rest of Hood's force remained at Columbia.

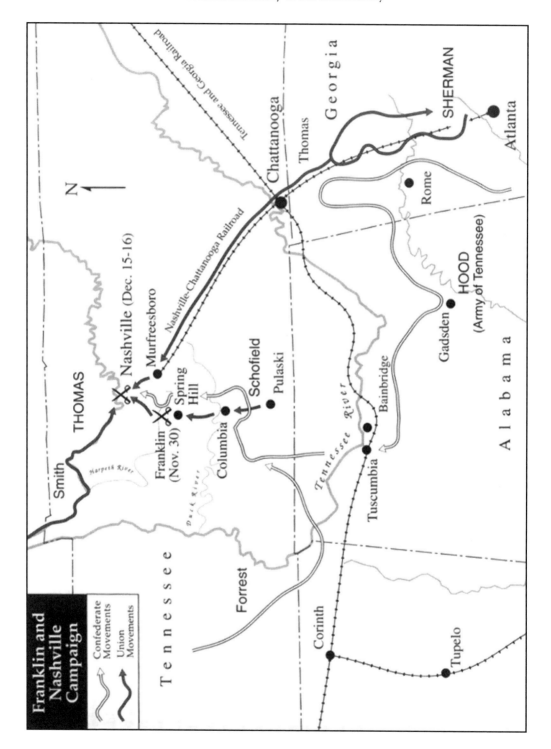

Franklin and Nashville Campaign
Confederate Movements
Union Movements

At this point confusion became the order of the day. Hood's staff simply broke down, and his control of the army dissolved. The following day, with some order finally restored, they had no choice but to regroup and press on to Franklin.

On November 30 Hood threw his army into a massive frontal assault against General Schofield's army at Franklin. Hood's men were initially successful, but strong Union reinforcements finally pushed them back. That night Schofield pulled his forces back and continued his march to Nashville. Hood lost over 5,000 men in this engagement, including twelve general officers and 55 regimental commanders.

Hood found himself in a dilemma. He could not now turn and pursue Sherman across Georgia, yet his army was too weak to attack Schofield at Nashville. Perhaps he could entrench and wait for Schofield to attack him.

General George H. Thomas, meanwhile, continued to organize his force in Nashville. He wanted to build an army that could thoroughly destroy Hood's force once and for all.

On December 15 Thomas' Federals launched an overwhelming attack against Hood's left flank. The Confederates fell back to the Brentwood Hills. On the morning of the sixteenth Thomas assaulted Hood's new line, opening with a massive artillery barrage that pulverized the southerners. That afternoon the Confederates fled southward. They finally retreated all the way to Tupelo, Mississippi.

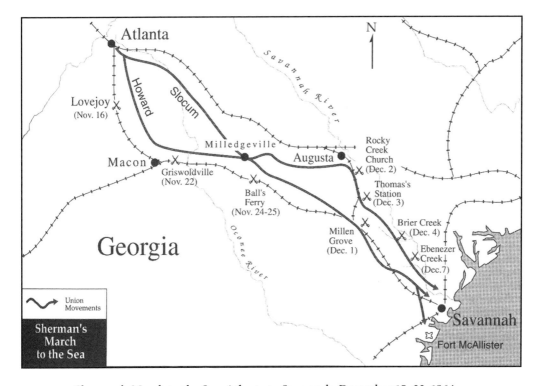

Sherman's March to the Sea, Atlanta to Savannah, December 15–22, 1864.

*Opposite*: Franklin and Nashville, Tennessee, November 30–December 16, 1864.

Hood's Franklin and Nashville campaign had been a total disaster, and essentially destroyed the Army of Tennessee. (See battle map.)

**Sherman's March to the Sea, Atlanta to Savannah, November–December, 1864:** In early November Sherman dispatched General Thomas to Nashville to grapple with General Hood should he decide to turn northwest in order to menace Tennessee. After putting the torch to Atlanta on November 12, rendering it uninhabitable, Sherman then divided his 62,000-man army into two wings to march eastward in parallel columns. They would forage for food and grain, he ordered, and there would be no destruction of personal property. Negro slaves who could be used as laborers would be allowed to follow the army, but there would be no mass liberation of slaves.

On November 15 his army marched out of Atlanta. They encountered little opposition, simply women and children, and food was plentiful. On December 10 he captured Fort McAllister, just south of Savannah, and on December 22 he captured Savannah. Now he was in position to move north and cooperate with Grant in a campaign to destroy the Army of Northern Virginia. (See battle map.)

# 5

# Battle Flags

## *The Cary Girls and the First Immortal Battle Flags*

From the very beginning many southerners agreed that the Stars and Bars did not quite satisfy their tastes in what a national flag should be. Mainly, it too closely resembled the Stars and Stripes, especially when hanging limply. This fact led to some unfortunate consequences once the real fighting began.

Indeed, there were numerous instances reported of young men (from both sides) who had attempted to rally 'round the flag during the confusion of battle only to find that they had rallied 'round the wrong flag, sometimes with devastating results.

Soldiers from both sides complained that during the heat and smoke of battle it was truly difficult to distinguish the Stars and Bars from the Stars and Stripes.

Thus, following First Manassas in July of 1861, both generals Joe Johnston and P. G. T. Beauregard, who shared command of Confederate forces at First Manassas, wrote the Confederate Congress requesting a new, and more distinctive, flag.

For a while nothing was done. Indeed, Congressman William Porcher Miles responded to General Beauregard that Congress had a problem complying with their requests for a new flag because "it is impossible to tear people away from a desire to retain some reminiscence of the United States flag." This was hardly the reply that Johnston and Beauregard wanted to hear. Thus Johnston took the bull by the horns and issued a general request for suggestions for a new southern banner.

It seems fitting that the suggestion rendered by none other than Colonel Miles, who had earlier submitted his design to the Confederate Congress in March of '61 and was now serving on Beauregard's staff, should have been chosen as the very best. His flag featured a red field divided diagonally by a blue St. Andrew's cross on which were placed thirteen stars, one for each of the eleven seceded states, plus the two border states, Missouri and Maryland.

General Johnston immediately fell in love with this simple yet beautiful design, and then modified it himself by suggesting that this new flag should be square instead of oblong. (Johnston made this suggestion simply in hopes of saving fabric.)

Johnston then submitted this design to the War Department, which immediately granted approval, and on October 1, 1861, the illustrious Battle Flag of the Confederacy became a reality.

Strangely enough, the Confederate Congress never formally adopted the battle flag as the official banner of the Confederacy. But that mattered little, for within months the battle flag had captured the hearts of soldiers and citizens throughout the Eastern Theater of war. One authority referred to this banner as "the most perfect flag ever designed." (Oddly enough, during the war this flag was referred to not as the Battle Flag but as the Southern Cross.)

As noted above, the flag was square in shape. The naval ensign was rectangular. Today it is the naval ensign that is inevitably flown by various groups and agencies in the mistaken belief that they are honoring the old battle flag.

It should be pointed out that, in keeping with the very best romantic southern traditions, the first three of these battle flags were made not in a grimy Richmond factory, but by three beautiful young ladies who were visiting with the Beauregards at headquarters in Centerville, Virginia, when the War Department approved the design for the new banner. These young ladies were the Cary cousins, Hetty, Jennie and Constance. They were the belles of Richmond and referred to as "the Cary Invincibles." In time Constance would marry Burton Harrison, secretary to President Jefferson Davis, and following the war she would become a novelist of some note. In later years, in an article entitled "A Virginia Girl in the First Year of the War," published in *The Century Illustrated Monthly Magazine,* Constance would recall:

**General John Pegram** (National Archives)     **Hetty Cary** (Virginia Historical Society)

*The lovely Miss Hetty Cary and her cousins, Jenny and Constance Cary, used fabric from their own pink dresses to make the first three battle flags for the Confederacy. In January of '65, Hetty, the belle of Richmond society, married General John Pegram, an event which aroused so much interest that even Mary Todd Lincoln's sister came down from Washington to attend the wedding. Eighteen days later, on February 6, Hetty attended Pegram's funeral following his fatal wounding at Hatcher's Run. After the war Hetty married a college professor and spent the rest of her life touring and teaching in Europe.*

**Constance Cary** (Virginia Historical Society)    **Jennie Cary** (Virginia Historical Society)

> Another incident of note, during the autumn of '61, was that to my cousins, Hetty and Jennie Cary, and to me was entrusted the making of the first three battle flags of the Confederacy. They were jaunty squares of scarlet crossed with dark blue edged with white, the cross bearing stars to indicate the number of the seceded States. We set our best stitches upon them, edged them with golden fringes, and when they were finished, dispatched one to Johnston, another to Beauregard, and the third to Earl Van Dorn, then commanding infantry at Manassas. The banners were received with all possible enthusiasm; we were toasted, feted, and cheered abundantly. After two years, when Van Dorn had been killed in Tennessee, mine came back to me, tattered and storm-stained from long and honorable service in the field.

Since there was no material available for making flags, these girls took fabric from their own silk dresses to make these superb banners. (Today, visitors to the Washington Artillery Museum in New Orleans, where these flags are on display, are surprised to find that these original flags are more of a feminine pink than martial red. But there was no other fabric available to the Cary girls at the time.)

These three battle flags were presented to the troops on November 28, Thanksgiving Day. Great parties were held in celebration of that memorable event, and a letter of gratitude from General Beauregard to the Cary girls was read. Indeed, a young officer in Van Dorn's command was so overcome with emotion that he sprang to his horse, drew his sword, and swore an oath that he would join in Van Dorn's promise to Constance Cary to drive the Yankees from her nearby home in Alexandria.

At this point, Jennie Cary, a native of Baltimore, stood and sang a song that she had recently composed. Entitled "Maryland, My Maryland," it remains one of the best

*Upon General Earl Van Dorn's death in 1863, this flag was returned to Miss Constance Cary. This banner is now on display at the Washington Artillery Museum in New Orleans.* (Museum of the Confederacy)

*The Battle Flag Hetty Cary presented to General Joseph Johnston. Fabric from the Cary girls' own dresses was used for this venture, and thus the first three Battle Flags appear more pink than red.* (Museum of the Confederacy)

known and most beloved songs to emerge from the War Between the States. (Jennie took her lyrics from a poem by Maryland native James Ryder Randall and set them to the tune of the old German favorite "O, Tannenbaum.")

Later, following the presentation of flags, soldiers and visitors alike were treated to a fine banquet. Toast after toast was offered to various friends of the Confederate army, so that by evening many of the South's finest were quite tipsy. Indeed, three of General Longstreet's top generals, in a show of drunken patriotism, mounted a shaky wooden table to lead the crowd in the singing of "Dixie." At that point the table suddenly collapsed and the gallant heroes of First Manassas tumbled unceremoniously to the ground. The crowd roared with laughter.

It was then that an aide called on General Kirby Smith to come out of his tent and give a talk to a smaller party of celebrants, where generals Johnston and Beauregard were in attendance. But the dour Smith refused, saying that he could not speak soberly to a drunken audience.

Years following the war the battle flag that Jennie Cary presented to General Beauregard would be used to drape the coffins of both Beauregard and Jefferson Davis.

## Battle Flags for the Army of Northern Virginia

In October of 1861 Confederate quartermaster Colin M. Selph charged three Richmond sewing circles with the noble task of fashioning 120 silk battle flags for the Army of Northern Virginia.

**The Sixth South Carolina Infantry Regiment.** *A part of General David R. Jones' Brigade, the Sixth South Carolina received their battle flag on November 28, 1861, in a ceremony that one soldier remembered as "the grandest time we ever had. We were drawn up in a hollow square and several speeches were made. The noise of the men was deafening."* (Confederate Relic Room, Columbia, S.C.)

In July of 1862 Richmond officially ordered the battle flag for the Army of Northern Virginia. Over the next two years these flags were produced in such quantities that entire divisions could be furnished with them at the same time. D. H. Hill's division received their new flags after Fredericksburg, A.P. Hill's division after Chancellorsville, and several other divisions after suffering heavy losses at Gettysburg.

**Battle Flag of the 18th Mississippi Infantry Regiment.** (The Museum of the Confederacy, Richmond. Photograph by Katherine Wetzel)

## Battle Flags in the South and West

Initially, the Battle Flag, or Southern Cross, was used primarily by Confederate Army units in the Eastern theater of war (the Army of Northern Virginia), while units in the Western and Southern theaters continued to use their old standards. Indeed, it was not until 1862–63 when generals Beauregard and Johnston were transferred to commands in the South and West, that the new flag was most reluctantly adopted (if at all) by armies in those theaters of war.

But even at that, Johnston was only partially successful in introducing the flag to the Army of Tennessee in 1863–64. Earl Van Dorn, the recipient of one of the original flags, had been in command of the Armies of the West before Johnston's arrival, and he had already designed his own distinctive battle flag, a red field bordered in gold with a gold crescent in the upper staff corner, the rest of the field studded with 13 gold stars. When Van Dorn's army moved to reinforce Beauregard's Army of the Mississippi after Shiloh, they took along their own flag, which continued in service throughout 1862.

To further complicate the flag situation, when Beauregard arrived in the West he found that General Leonidas Polk's troops had adopted as their battle flag a blue flag traversed by a red Saint George's Cross bearing eleven white stars. General Hardee's army had adopted a battle flag featuring a blue field bordered in white, with a white disk in its center. These armies refused to change battle flags.

## Beauregard Moves South

When General Beauregard took command of Confederate forces in Charleston in 1862 he found to his dismay that southern units scattered throughout the southeast, ignoring Richmond's directive to adapt the Southern Cross as their standard, were still using their old homemade flags and banners. He attempted to eliminate such flags and ordered the Charleston Clothing Depot to begin producing the new flag as a replacement. The following flags serve as examples of what Beauregard found upon his arrival in Charleston.

**The Marion Artillery of South Carolina.** *Named in memory of General Swamp Fox Marion, this flag bears symbols from the Revolution: the crescent moon, the palmetto tree and the fox.* (The South Carolina Confederate Relic Room, Columbia)

**The 27th South Carolina Infantry.** *Four South Carolina regiments had adopted flags of this general design, one recommended by the* Charleston Mercury. *The 27th took part in the Battle of Secessionville in March of '62, and the initials stand for the Charleston Light Infantry.* (The South Carolina Confederate Relic Room, Columbia)

**1st Florida Infantry Battalion.** *In February of 1862 Beauregard ordered a New Orleans sail maker to make battle flags for Braxton Bragg's Army of the Mississippi. The result was this interesting variation of the battle flag. It is oblong rather than square, and contains twelve six-pointed stars.* (The Confederate Museum, New Orleans)

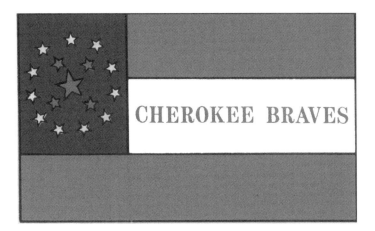

**First Cherokee Mounted Rifles:** *This daring unit was composed of Cherokees recruited from the Indian Territory (Oklahoma) in 1861. CSA Indian Commissioner General Albert Pike presented this flag to the Cherokees that same year. The five red stars within the circle of 11 white ones symbolize the Five Civilized Tribes (Cherokee, Creek, Chickasaw, Choctaw, and Seminole).* (Flags of the Confederacy)

**The Choctaw Volunteers:** *The unstrung bow symbolizes that the Choctaw are a peaceful people, but the arrows and hatchet suggest that they are prepared to defend themselves if necessary.* (Flags of the Confederacy)

## Confederate Naval Banners

Throughout the war the Confederate Navy designed its own official flags. At first the Navy simply used the Stars and Bars, but then on May 26, 1862, Secretary of the Navy Stephen R. Mallory authorized three new banners: a new ensign, the Navy Jack, and the Navy Pennant. The new ensign was nothing more than the Stainless Banner.

*An early version of the Stars and Bars flown by the C.S.S.* Virginia. *This banner would later be replaced with an 11-star flag, which the Vir-ginia was flying during her battle with the U.S.S.* Monitor *on March 9, 1862.* (Flags of the Confederacy)

*The* Virginia *flies the* **Stars and Bars** *during her clash with the* Monitor, *March 9, 1862.* (The Naval Historical Center)

## *The Stainless Banner*

Still, the Confederate Congress pushed on in its efforts to find and adopt a new national flag. On May 1, 1863, they did just that. This new banner featured the battle flag as the union (a square two-thirds the width of the flag), with a field of white. Traditionally, some have called it the Stainless Banner because of its large field of white, while others have called it the Jackson Flag because the first one made was used to drape the coffin of General Stonewall Jackson.

But this flag, like the Stars and Bars, did not enjoy much popularity with either the Confederate Army or with southerners in general. With its length twice its width, it simply did not look right. Worse, when hanging limp, with its large field of white, it appeared to be a flag of surrender. One can only imagine the confusion this could cause on the field of battle — to both sides. (Indeed, if the Confederate Congress was no better in determining southern policy than in adopting a national banner, then one wonders how the South managed to fight on so doggedly for four long years against the might of the Federal government. Apparently adopting a national banner did not stand high on the Confederate list of priorities.)

So for the next two years then the Stainless Banner was the official flag of the Confederacy, though no one liked it particularly, and few Confederate units ever flew it in combat, preferring their old battle flags to anything they'd seen either before or since.

The Second National Flag, called The Stainless Banner, *adopted May 1, 1863. (This particular banner was the head-quarters flag of General Robert F. Hoke.)* (N.C. Division of Archives and History, Raleigh)

General J. E. B. Stuart's Headquarters Flag. (Museum of the Confederacy, Richmond)

## *The Third National Banner*

On March 4, 1865, with the Confederacy on the verge of collapse, Congress adopted a new national banner. This one was an adaptation of the Stainless Banner but with the following differences: its width was two-thirds its length (instead of one-half), and the Battle Flag canton became a rectangle rather than a square. To eliminate its resemblance to a flag of surrender, a broad red vertical stripe was placed at the outer end of the flag. This banner was considered an improvement over the Stainless Banner, but the war ended before it could ever be put to use.

**The Third National Flag,** *adopted March 4, 1865, just prior to war's end.* (Flags of the Confederacy)

Sherman's army entered South Carolina in February of '65. Against a southern army composed mainly of Fighting Joe Wheeler's cavalry and women and children, Sherman's bummers raped, murdered and robbed their way across the state. Mary Chestnut, in her *A Diary from Dixie,* reported that the roadways of Georgia and South Carolina were littered with the bodies of young black girls who had been raped and murdered by Sherman's army. Unfortunately, the South lost the war and thus could not bring war crimes charges against the leaders of the Union Army.

**The Headquarters Flag of General Joseph Johnston** *which he adopted as he fought Sherman across North Carolina.* (The Museum of the Confederacy, Richmond. Photograph by Katherine Wetzel)

**Father Abraham Ryan** (Maryland Historical Society)

**The Conquered Banner**
by Father Abraham Ryan
of Baltimore, Maryland

*Furl that banner, for 'tis weary;*
*Round its staff 'tis drooping dreary*
*Furl it, fold it — it is best;*
*For there's not a man to wave it,*
*And there's not a sword to save it,*
*And there's not one left to lave it*
*In the blood which heroes gave it;*
*Furl it, hide it — let it rest!*
*Furl that banner! True, 'tis gory,*
*Yet 'tis wreathed around with glory,*
*And 'twill live in song and story*
*Though its folds are in the dust;*
*For its fame on brightest pages,*
*Penned by poets and by sages,*
*Shall go sounding down the ages —*
*Furl its folds now we must.*

**"Furling the Banner"** (Richard Brooke, artist, from the collection of Alexander Craighead, West Point Museum)

# 6

# End of the War

By January of 1865 it was obvious to everyone, North and South, that the Confederacy was on the verge of collapse. After nearly four long years of all-out war, there were few provisions left to feed the army, southern factories were producing little, and almost all southern ports were now blockaded. As for military manpower, the Confederate Army was now accepting boys of fourteen and old men of sixty. In January the South decided to tap its last resource, the slave, promising freedom to those who would enlist. But the law did not go into effect until March 20, too late for it to show any results. The situation was indeed desperate. Still, the Confederacy fought doggedly on, subsisting on nothing more than courage and determination.

By now only two theaters of war counted, Virginia and the Carolinas. General Lee's Army of Northern Virginia had dwindled to less than 50,000 men, and now they were immobilized at Richmond by the Army of the Potomac with 110,000 men. In Georgia and South Carolina Sherman was on the march northward with a force of 60,000. As an indication of President Davis' desperation, on February 23 he put aside personal animosities and restored General Joe Johnston to command the 20,000 southern soldiers in the Carolinas.

At Petersburg, General Grant began the campaign that he hoped would end the war. He would extend his lines westward and cut the last railroad lines that supplied Confederates hemmed in at Petersburg and Richmond. On March 29 Grant dispatched Sheridan's cavalry to accomplish that goal. General Lee moved quickly to meet the threat, and on April 1, at Five Forks, fifteen miles west of Petersburg, General George Pickett attempted to turn back the Federals. But after a daylong fight Pickett's badly outnumbered southerners were forced to withdraw.

At this point it became obvious to General Lee that further defense of Richmond was no longer feasible, and thus he decided to evacuate the capital as quickly as possible. Aware of his enemy's intentions, Grant ordered a massive assault against southern lines at Petersburg on April 2. But again the Confederate defenders of those lines managed to turn back the Federals, giving Lee time for an orderly withdrawal and allowing Jefferson Davis and his Cabinet to escape from the doomed Richmond.

Lee's plan was to move his scattered army of some 58,000 men to rendezvous at Amelia Courthouse, then move southward and join Johnston's army in North Carolina where together, with an army of 65,000 men, they could confront Sherman. And thus during the first week of April the Army of Northern Virginia began a desperate race southward with the Army of the Potomac in hot pursuit. Frequent minor battles ensued during Lee's last ditch escape attempt (General A. P. Hill was killed at

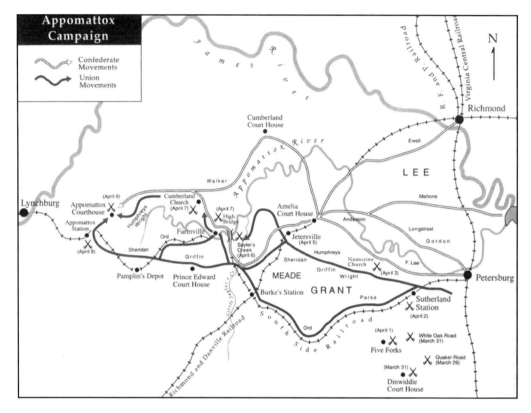

**Appomattox Court House, Virginia, April 9, 1865.**

Saylors Creek on April 3), but on April 7 Sheridan managed to place his brigades in front of Lee's retreating army at Appomattox, sixty miles west of Petersburg. On April 8 Grant sent a message to General Lee pointing out his hopeless situation and proposing that he surrender. Lee, his alternatives exhausted, asked Grant for terms.

Thus on April 9 generals Lee and Grant met at Appomattox Court House to discuss just how the fighting could finally end. Grant, of course, military concerns aside, was also forced to follow Federal War Department guidelines for surrender. Two weeks later, in Greensboro, N.C., General Sherman would ignore War Department guidelines when negotiating terms of surrender with Joe Johnston. As a result, President Andrew Johnson furiously tore up their surrender agreement and ordered Sherman to again meet with Johnston and inform him that their agreement was null and void. Thus Sherman was placed in the embarrassing position of again having to sit down with Johnston and renegotiate his surrender.

Casualties for the Appomattox campaign totaled 9,000 for the Federal Army and 28,000, including desertions, for the Confederates. Lee surrendered 30,000 men.

Still, Grant's terms were fairly lenient under the circumstances: he asked that the soldiers of the Army of Northern Virginia give their word that they would not take up arms again until properly exchanged; the men could keep their sidearms and muskets; and they could keep their horses and mules. Then, as a further sign of goodwill, Grant ordered that rations immediately be furnished to Lee's 30,000 starving soldiers.

For the Army of Northern Virginia the war had finally ended. (See battle map.)

Back in Richmond, meanwhile, on the night of April 2 Jefferson Davis and his Cabinet (except for Secretary of War John C. Breckinridge) boarded a train for Danville, where Davis planned to establish a new Confederate capital. A week later, however, on April 10, word reached Davis that General Lee had surrendered. Thus Davis and his Cabinet fled to Greensboro, N.C., where Joe Johnston's army was now based. Once there, Davis informed Johnston and Beauregard that he wanted their soldiers to fight to the last man. But Johnston objected, stating that "it would be the greatest of crimes" to continue the war when the end was inevitable. At that point Davis reluctantly agreed that Johnston should ask Sherman for surrender terms.

With the railroads now destroyed, Davis and his Cabinet were forced to take to horses and wagons as they fled southward. Now it was his plan to make their way to Texas, and there, supported by the army of Kirby Smith, the Confederacy could continue the war indefinitely. Escorted by Fighting Joe Wheeler's cavalry, Davis and his entourage traveled several hundred miles southward, but then, on May 10, they were finally captured near Irwinville, Georgia. Davis was immediately arrested and imprisoned at Fortress Monroe. For all practical purposes, though several generals in the Western Theater still refused to surrender their armies, the arrest of Jefferson Davis marked the end of the southern Confederacy.

By January of '65 it had become obvious to all that the Confederacy could not hold out much longer. Grant had Lee's army pinned down in the Richmond-Petersburg area, while Sherman was tightening the noose as his army sped northward, almost unopposed, through Georgia and the Carolinas. And now, to add to Jefferson Davis' problems, it appeared that the Federals might capture Wilmington, N.C., the last port on the Atlantic seaboard still open to the South.

**Fort Fisher, N.C., January 15, 1865:** And that is just what the Federals had in mind. To achieve that end, they would capture Fort Fisher, located near the mouth of the Cape Fear River, which guarded the approach to Wilmington. The attack was to be a coordinated effort between General A. H. Terry's 8,000 Federal infantry and Admiral Porter's North Atlantic Squadron. There were only 1,200 Confederates guarding the fort, and thus its commander urgently requested reinforcements from General Braxton Bragg. For reasons known only to himself, Bragg refused to send reinforcements. The attack began on the night of January 15 with a heavy naval bombardment. Then came Terry's troops, and the beleaguered southerners had no choice but to surrender. With the fall of Fort Fisher, the Federal fleet moved on to blockade Wilmington, and now the Confederacy was effectively isolated from the entire world. (See battle map.) (Indeed, following the war Vice President Alexander H. Stephens would write: "The fall of this fort was one of the greatest disasters which had befallen our cause from the beginning of the war — not excepting the fall of Vicksburg or Atlanta.")

**Sherman's Carolinas Campaign, January–April 1865:** Both Lincoln and Grant suggested that Sherman transport his troops by water to Virginia once he had captured Savannah, and there were ships waiting there for that purpose. But Sherman requested permission to march across the Carolinas just as he had done in Georgia, and Lincoln and Grant, aware that the Army of Tennessee had just been destroyed at Nashville, agreed to that request. This plan gave Sherman the opportunity to apply what he called "total war" to the Carolinas, especially South Carolina where the war had begun.

From Savannah Sherman and his 60,000 bummers moved into the Palmetto State. His left wing was commanded by General Henry Slocum, the right by General O. O. Howard. General Judson Kilpatrick was in charge of the cavalry.

On February 12 the Federals occupied Orangeburg, then five days later, on February 17, Columbia was in Federal hands. Indeed, for several generations now Carolinians have remembered February 17 as a night of horror as Sherman's drunken bummers engaged in unrestrained burning, looting and general debauchery throughout the Columbia area. The president of the South Carolina College, for example, informed Sherman that the college had been turned into a military hospital and that over a hundred wounded Union soldiers were being treated there. Sherman had armed guards placed at all the entrances to the college, but still his bummers managed to burn one of the hospital buildings.

At Cheraw, Sherman's last stop in South Carolina, he learned that General Joe Johnston had replaced Beauregard as commander of southern forces in Georgia and the Carolinas. Based on long experience, he suspected that Johnston would somehow manage to unite his forces and fight a final battle at a place of his choosing.

On March 8 the Union Army entered North Carolina and made for Fayetteville, where General Wade Hampton and his cavalry awaited their arrival. There, in a brief

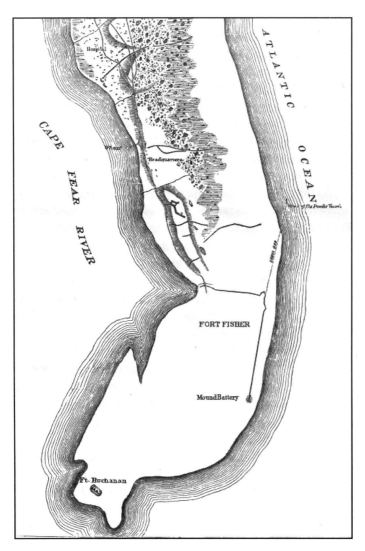

Fort Fisher, N.C., January 15, 1865.

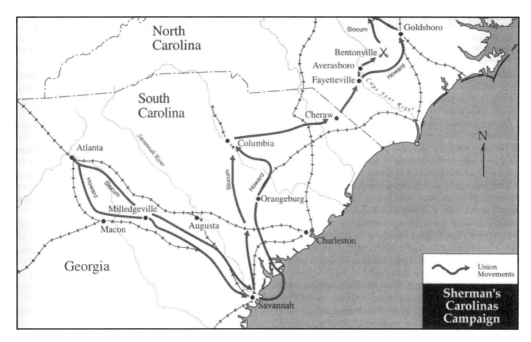

**Sherman's Carolinas Campaign, January–April 1865.**

battle of only several hours' duration, Hampton scattered Kilpatrick's surprised cavalry, while Kilpatrick himself narrowly escaped being captured. That night Hampton, Joe Wheeler and the remnants of General Hardee's army joined forces.

On March 19 Sherman, who had allowed his army to become strung out over a large area, watched apprehensively as Joe Johnston, who had managed to unite his own scattered force of 21,000 men, came close to crushing Sherman's 14th Corps at Bentonville. But Federal reinforcements forced Johnston to retire to Smithfield, ten miles to the west. And that, for all practical purposes, was the Confederacy's final effort to resist Sherman's army.

Three days later Sherman arrived in Goldsboro, completing his march through Georgia and the Carolinas. Now he had only to dictate surrender terms to Joe Johnston and the war in the South and West would be at an end. (See battle map.)

Johnston met with Sherman on April 18, and Sherman, excited at the prospect of ending the war on the spot, offered terms that were far more generous than those Grant offered Lee. In addition to accepting the surrender of Johnston's army, Sherman stated that the executive of the United States would recognize the governments of the southern states when their officers and legislatures took the oath prescribed by the Constitution; that the federal courts would be re-established; that the political rights and franchises of the people of all the states would be guaranteed; and that no one would be disturbed by reason of the late war. President Andrew Johnson immediately rejected this agreement and informed a furious Sherman to give Johnston the same terms Grant had given Lee. This was done, and on April 26, 1865, Johnston surrendered all the Confederate forces in his command. The War Between the States was over.

**Captain James I. Waddell**: *Commander of the C.S.S.* Shenandoah, *he finally surrendered his flag on November 6, 1865, thus making Waddell the last CSA officer to officially surrender his banner to the enemy.* (Official U.S. Navy Photograph)

Captain James I. Waddell, commander of the Confederate cruiser *Shenandoah*, did not receive the shocking news that the war had ended until August 2, 1865. At that point, not quite sure what he should do with himself, his crew or his ship, he solved the problem by immediately sailing for England. On the morning of November 6, 1865, Waddell slowly maneuvered his cruiser alongside the British man-of-war *Donegal* in Liverpool harbor. Soon a British officer came aboard the Confederate cruiser and officially informed Waddell that he must surrender his ship.

Captain Waddell went to his cabin, donned his dress uniform, then returned on deck amid the silence of his assembled officers and seamen, standing now at rigid attention. He then delivered a short speech thanking all for their courage and loyal service to the Confederacy. At the conclusion of his talk, he gave a slight nod to the quartermaster who stepped forward and, as the assembled openly began to weep, the last flag of the Confederacy was slowly lowered. Thus it is said that the *Shenandoah*'s New Ensign was the last flag to be officially flown in the service of the Confederacy.

*Looking up Main Street from the State House in Columbia, S.C., following a terrifying night of debauchery, looting and burning as Sherman's drunken bummers ran wild through the city.* (Library of Congress)

*Churches, schools and hospitals made inviting targets for Sherman's bummers as they swept through Georgia and the Carolinas late in the war.* (Library of Congress)

**General Robert E. Lee's farewell address** *to his Army of Northern Virginia.* (The Museum of the Confederacy, Richmond)

*Opposite:* *In this Louis Guillaume painting General Robert E. Lee surrenders to General Ulysses S. Grant in the parlor of the McLean House at Appomattox Court House on April 12, 1865. (In fact, Lee and Grant sat at separate tables, about five feet apart.) Grant's terms were fairly generous: Confederate soldiers would be paroled, not sent to prison camps; officers could keep their sidearms and personal property; and all could keep their horses and mules. He also offered to provide rations for Lee's army, an offer which was gratefully accepted.* (Appomattox Court House National Historical Park)

FINALE of the "JEFF DAVIS DIE-NASTY."
"Last Scene of all, that ends this strange eventful History."

*In April of 1865, President Andrew Johnson announced his conviction that the Confederate Secret Service was behind the assassination of President Abraham Lincoln, an opinion shared by many throughout the nation (as indicated in the above political cartoon). It was known, for example, that both John Wilkes Booth and John Surratt were paid agents of the Confederate Secret Service, and it is a fact that a Confederate bank draft drawn on a Montreal bank for $1,000 was found on the body of John Wilkes Booth, and it is also a fact that Jacob Thompson fled the country rather than face questions following the assassination. Still, a Federal investigation could find no connection whatsoever between the Confederate government and the president's assassination. Following the death of Lafayette Baker, head of the Federal Secret Service, papers were found which strongly implicated both Baker and Secretary of War Edwin Stanton in President Lincoln's assassination.* (Library of Congress)

**John Wilkes Booth** (National Archives)   **John Surratt** (National Archives)

*Despite the Federal government's finding that the Confederate Secret Service was not implicated in the assassination of President Lincoln, it is a fact that both John Wilkes Booth and John Surratt were paid agents of the Confederate Secret Service, and both served as couriers between Montreal and Richmond. Indeed, rumors persist to this very day that Federal Secretary of War Edwin Stanton and his Secret Service director, Lafayette Baker, were deeply involved in the assassination conspiracy.*

*The accused assassins, having been found guilty by a military court, were hanged. (L–R): Mary Surratt, Lewis Powell, David Herold, and George Atzerodt. (National Archives)*

**"The Lost Cause"** *(Currier and Ives, 1871). This print depicts all too well the tragic situations faced by so many Confederate soldiers on their return home after four long years of warfare.* (West Point Museum)

**President Jefferson Davis died at the age of 81** *on December 6, 1889. Over 10,000 mourners filed past his coffin here in front of the Supreme Court bench in the Alabama state capitol building in Montgomery. His coffin was draped with the same battle flag that had draped the coffin of General P. G. T. Beauregard.* (Fouts Commercial Photography)

*Varina Davis initially chose a vault in Metarie Cemetery in New Orleans as a temporary resting place for President Davis' remains. Then, on May 27, 1893, she had her husband's body removed to Hollywood Cemetery in Richmond, the final resting place of thousands of Confederate soldiers. In the scene above Davis' funeral bier is seen en route from Montgomery to Atlanta. The coffin and horses were decorated in purple. A gold crown sits at the peak of the caisson's canopy.* (Fouts Commercial Photography)

**Lee as President of Washington College,** 1869. (Washington and Lee University)

*In this memorial sheet music, published by Charles Bayly of Baltimore in 1870, Bayly mourns the death of the general, not the college president.* (Lincoln Library and Museum)

*The noble Lee finally at rest in the Lee Chapel at Washington and Lee University.* (Washington and Lee University)

### Robert E. Lee
By Julia Ward Howe

*A gallant foe in the fight,*
*A brother when the fight was o'er,*
*The hand that led the host with might*
*The blessed torch of learning bore.*
*No shriek of shells nor roll of drums,*
*No challenge fierce, resounding far,*
*When reconciling Wisdom comes*
*To heal the cruel wounds of war.*
*Thought may the minds of men divide,*
*Love makes the heart of nations one,*
*And so, thy soldier's grave beside,*
*We honor thee, Virginia's son.*

# Index

Boldface indicates photographs, illustrations or maps.

DATE DUE

GAYLORD                                    PRINTED IN U.S.A.